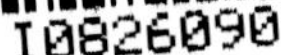
I0826090

THE LIFE

OF

COL. JAMES GARDINER,

WHO WAS SLAIN AT

THE BATTLE OF PRESTONPANS,

SEPTEMBER 21, 1745.

BY

P. DODDRIDGE, D. D.

Justior alter
Nec pietate fuit, nec bello major et armis. VIRG.

PHILADELPHIA:
PRESBYTERIAN BOARD OF PUBLICATION,
No. 265 CHESTNUT STREET.

LIFE

OF

COL. JAMES GARDINER.

CHAPTER I.

PARENTAGE AND EARLY DAYS.

WHEN I promised the public some larger account of the life and character of this illustrious person, than I could conveniently insert in my sermon on the sad occasion of his death, I was secure, that if Providence continued my capacity of writing, I should not wholly disappoint the expectation; for I was furnished with a variety of particulars which appeared to me worthy of general notice, in consequence of that intimate friendship with which he had honoured me during the last six years of his life—a friendship which led him to open his heart to me, in repeated conversations, with an unbounded confidence, (as he then assured me, beyond what he had used with any other man living,) so far as religious experiences were concerned; and I had also received several very valuable letters from him during the time of our absence from each other, which contained most genuine and edifying traces of his Christian character. But I hoped further to learn many valuable particulars from the papers of his own closet, and from his letters to other friends, as well as from what they more circumstantially knew concerning him. I therefore determined to delay the execution of my promise till I could enjoy these advantages for performing it in the most satisfactory manner; nor have I, on the whole, reason to regret that determination.

I shall not trouble the reader with all the causes which concurred to retard these expected assistances for almost a whole year. The chief of them was the tedious languishing illness of his afflicted lady, through whose hands it was proper the papers should pass; together with the confusion into which the rebels had thrown them when they ransacked his seat at Bankton, where most of them were deposited. But having now received such of them as have escaped their rapacious hands, and could conveniently be collected and transmitted, I set myself with the greatest pleasure to perform what I esteem not merely a tribute of gratitude to the memory of my invaluable friend, (though never was the memory of any mortal man more precious and sacred to me,) but of duty to God, and to my fellow-creatures; for I have a most cheerful hope that the narrative I am now to write will, under the divine blessing, be a means of spreading, what of all things in the world, every benevolent heart will most desire to spread, a warm and lively sense of religion.

My own heart has been so much edified and animated by what I have read in the memoirs of persons who have been eminent for wisdom and piety, that I cannot but wish the treasure may be more and more increased; and I would hope the world may gather the like valuable fruits from the life I am now attempting, not only as it will contain very singular circumstances, which may excite general curiosity, but as it comes attended with some other particular advantages.

The reader is here to survey a character of such eminent and various goodness as might demand veneration, and inspire him with a desire of imitating it too, had it appeared in the obscurest rank; but it will surely command some peculiar regard, when viewed in so elevated and important a station, especially as it shone, not in ecclesiastical, but *military* life, where the temptations are so many, and the prevalence of the contrary character so great, that it may seem no inconsiderable praise and felicity to be free from dissolute vice, and to retain what in most other professions might be esteemed only *a mediocrity of virtue.* It may surely, with the highest justice, be expected that the title and bravery of Colonel Gardiner will invite many of our officers and soldiers, to whom his name has been long honourable and dear, to peruse this account of him with some peculiar attention; in consequence of which it may be a means of increasing the number, and brightening the character of those who are already adorning their office, their country, and their religion; and of reclaiming those who will see what they ought to be, rather than what they are. On the whole, to the gentlemen of the sword I would particularly offer these memoirs, as theirs by so distinguished a title; yet I am firmly persuaded there are *none* whose office is so sacred, or whose proficiency in the religious life is so advanced, but they may find something to demand their thankfulness, and to awaken their emulation.

COLONEL JAMES GARDINER was the son of Capt. Patrick Gardiner of the family of Torwood-head, by Mrs. Mary Hodge of the family of Gladsmuir. The captain, who was master of a handsome estate, served many years in the army of king William and queen Anne, and died abroad with the British forces in Germany, soon after the battle of Hochstett, through the fatigues he underwent in the duties of that celebrated campaign. He had a company in the regiment of foot once commanded by Colonel Hodge, his valiant brother-in-law, who was slain at the head of that regiment (my memorial from Scotland says) at the battle of Steenkirk, which was fought in the year 1692.

Mrs. Gardiner, our colonel's mother, was a lady of very respectable character; but it pleased God to exercise her with very uncommon trials; for she not only lost her husband and her brother in the service of their country, as before related, but also her eldest son, Mr. Robert Gardiner, on the day which completed the 16th year of his age, at the siege of Namur, in 1695. But there is great reason to believe that God blessed these various and heavy afflictions, as the means of forming her to that eminent degree of piety which will render her memory honourable as long as it continues.

Her second son, the worthy person of whom I am now to give a more particular account, was born at Carriden, in Linlithgowshire, on the 10th of January, A. D. 1687–8,—the memorable year of that glorious revolution which he justly esteemed among the happiest of all events; so that when he was slain in defence of those liberties which God then, by so gracious a providence, rescued from utter destruction, i. e. on the 21st of September 1745, he was aged 57 years, 8 months, and 11 days.

The annual return of his birth-day was observed by him in the latter and better years of his life, in a manner very different from what is commonly practised; for, instead of making it a day of festivity, I am told he rather distinguished it as a season of more than ordinary humiliation before God—both in commemoration of those mercies which he received in the first opening of life, and under an affectionate sense, as well of his long alienation from the great Author and support of his being, as of the many imperfections which he lamented in the best of his days and services.

I have not met with many things remarkable concerning the early days of his life, only that his mother took care to instruct him, with great tenderness and affection, in the principles of true Christianity. He was also trained up in humane literature, at the school at Linlithgow, where he made a very considerable progress in the languages. I remember to have heard him quote some passages of the Latin classics very pertinently; though his employment in life, and the various turns which his mind took under different impulses in succeeding years, prevented him from cultivating such studies.

The good effects of his mother's prudent and exemplary care were not so conspicuous as she wished and hoped, in the earlier part of her son's life; yet there is great reason to believe they were not entirely lost. As they were probably the occasion of many convictions which in his younger years were overborne, so I doubt not, that when religious impressions took that strong hold of his heart which they afterwards did, that stock of knowledge which had been so early laid up in his mind, was found of considerable service. And I have heard them make the observation, as an encouragement to parents, and other pious friends, to do their duty, and to hope for those good consequences of it which may not immediately appear.

Could his mother, or a very religious aunt, (of whose good instructions and exhortations I have often heard him speak with pleasure,) have prevailed, he would not have thought of a military life, from which it is no wonder these ladies endeavoured to dissuade him, considering the mournful experience they had of the dangers attending it, and the dear relatives they had lost already by it. But it suited his taste; and the ardour of his spirit, animated by the persuasions of a friend who greatly urged it,* was not to be restrained. Nor will the reader wonder that, thus excited and supported, it easily overbore their tender remonstrances, when he knows that this lively youth fought three duels before he attained to the stature of a man; in one of which, when he was but eight years old, he received from a boy much older than himself, a wound in his right cheek, the scar of which was always very apparent. The false sense of honour which instigated him to it, might seem indeed something excusable in those unripened years, and considering the profession of his

* I suppose this to have been Brigadier-General Rue, who had from his childhood a peculiar affection for him.

father, brother, and uncle; but I have often heard him mention this rashness with that regret which the reflection would naturally give to so wise and good a man in the maturity of life. And I have been informed that, after his remarkable conversion, he declined accepting a challenge, with this calm and truly great reply, which, in a man of his experienced bravery, was exceedingly graceful: "I fear sinning, though you know I do not fear fighting."

CHAPTER II.

BATTLE OF RAMILLIES.

He served first as a cadet, which must have been very early; and then, at fourteen years old, he bore an ensign's commission in a Scotch regiment in the Dutch service, in which he continued till the year 1702, when (if my information be right) he received an ensign's commission from queen Anne, which he bore in the battle of Ramillies, being then in the nineteenth year of his age. In this ever-memorable action he received a wound in his mouth by a musket-ball, which has often been reported to be the occasion of his conversion. That report was a mistaken one; but as some very remarkable circumstances attended this affair, which I have had the pleasure of hearing more than once from his own mouth, I hope my readers will excuse me, if I give him so uncommon a story at large.

Our young officer was of a party in the forlorn hope, and was commanded on what seemed almost a desperate service, to dispossess the French of the church-yard at Ramillies, where a considerable number of them were posted to remarkable advantage. They succeeded much better than was expected; and it may well be supposed that Mr. Gardiner, who had before been in several encounters, and had the view of making his fortune to animate the natural intrepidity of his spirit, was glad of such an opportunity of signalizing himself. Accordingly he had planted his colours on an advanced ground; and while he was calling to his men, (probably in that horrid language which is so peculiar a disgrace to our soldiery, and so absurdly common on such occasions of extreme danger,) he received into his mouth a shot, which, without beating out of any of his teeth, or touching the fore part of his tongue, went through his neck, and came out about an inch and a half on the left side of the *vertebræ*. Not feeling at first the pain of the stroke, he wondered what was become of the ball, and in the wildness of his surprise began to suspect he had swallowed it; but falling soon after, he traced the passage of it by his finger, when he could discover it in no other way; which I mention as one circumstance, among many which occur, to make it probable that the greater part of those who fall in battle by these instruments of death, feel very little anguish from the most mortal wounds.

This accident happened about five or six in the evening, on the 23d of May, 1706; and the army, pursuing its advantages against the French, without ever regarding the wounded, (which was, it seems, the Duke of Marlborough's constant method,) our young officer lay all night on the field, agitated, as may well be supposed, with a great variety of thoughts. He assured me, that when he reflected upon the circumstance of his wound, that a ball should, as he then conceived it, go through his head without killing him, he thought God had preserved him by a miracle; and therefore assuredly concluded that he should live, abandoned and desperate as his state seemed to be. Yet (which to me appeared very astonishing) he had little thoughts of humbling himself before God, and returning to him after the wanderings of a life so licentiously begun. But, expecting to recover, his mind was taken up with contrivances to secure his gold, of which he had a good deal about him; and he had recourse to a very odd expedient, which proved successful. Expecting to be stripped, he first took out a handful of that clotted gore of which he was frequently obliged to clear his mouth, or he would have been choked; and putting it into his left hand, he took out his money, which I think was about 19 pistoles, and shutting his hand, and besmearing the back part of it with blood, he kept in this position till the blood dried in such a manner that his hand could not easily fall open, though any sudden surprise should happen, in which he might lose the presence of mind which that concealment otherwise would have required.

In the morning the French, who were masters of that spot, though their forces were defeated at some distance, came to plunder the slain; and seeing him to appearance almost expiring, one of them was just applying a sword to his breast, to destroy the little remainder of life, when, in the critical moment, upon which all the extraordinary events of such a life as his afterwards proved, were suspended, a Cordelier who attended the plunderers interposed, (taking him by his dress for a Frenchman) and said, "Do not kill that poor child." Our young soldier heard all that passed, though he was not able to speak one word; and, opening his eyes, made a sign for something to drink. They gave him a sup of some spirituous liquor which happened to be at hand, by which he said he found a more sensible refreshment than he could remember from anything he had tasted either before or since. Then signifying to the friar to lean down his ear to his mouth, he employed the first efforts of his feeble breath in telling him (what, alas! was a contrived falsehood) that he was a nephew to the governor of Huy, a neutral town in the neighbourhood; and that if he could take any method of conveying him thither, he did not doubt but his uncle would liberally reward him. He had indeed a friend at Huy, who I think was governor, and, if I mistake not, had been acquainted with the captain, his father, from whom he expected a kind reception; but the relation was only pretended. On hearing this, they laid him on a sort of hand-barrow, and sent him by a file of musqueteers towards the place; but the men lost their way, and, towards the evening, got into a wood in which they were obliged to continue all night. The poor patient's wound being still undressed, it is not to be wondered at that by this time it raged violently. The anguish of it engaged him earnestly to beg that they would either kill him outright, or leave him there to die without the torture of any further motion; and indeed they were obliged to rest for a considerable time, on account of their own weariness. Thus he spent the second night in the open air, without any thing more than a common bandage to staunch the blood. He has often mentioned it as a most astonishing providence that he did not bleed to death, which, under God, he ascribed to the remarkable coldness of these two nights.

Judging it quite unsafe to attempt carrying him to Huy, from whence they were now several miles distant, his convoy took him early in the morning to a convent in the neighbourhood, where he was hospitably received, and treated with great kindness and tenderness. But the cure of his wound was committed to an ignorant barber-surgeon who lived near the house, the best shift that could then be made, at a time when it may easily be supposed persons of ability in their profession had their hands full of employment. The tent which this artist applied, was almost like a peg driven into the wound; and gentlemen of skill and experience, when they came to hear of the manner in which he was treated, wondered how he could possibly survive such management. But by the blessing of God on these applications, rough as they were, he recovered in a few months. The Lady Abbess, who called him her son, treated him with the affection and care of a mother; and he always declared that every thing which he saw within these walls, was conducted with the strictest decency and decorum. He received a great many devout admonitions from the ladies there, and they would fain have persuaded him to acknowledge what they thought so miraculous a deliverance, by embracing the *Catholic faith*, as they were pleased to call it. But they could not succeed; for though no religion lay near his heart, yet he had too much of the spirit of a gentleman lightly to change that form of religion which he wore, as it were loose about him; as well as too much good sense to swallow those monstrous absurdities of Popery which immediately presented themselves to him, unacquainted as he was with the niceties of the controversy.

CHAPTER III.

MILITARY PREFERMENTS.

WHEN his liberty was regained by an exchange of prisoners, and his health thoroughly established, he was far from rendering unto the Lord according to that wonderful display of divine mercy which he had experienced. I know very little of the particulars of those wild, thoughtless and wretched years which lay between the 19th and 30th of his life; except that he frequently experienced the divine goodness in renewed instances, particularly in preserving him in several hot military actions, in all which he never received so much as a wound after this, forward as he was in tempting danger; and yet that all these years were spent in an entire alienation from God, and in an eager pursuit of animal pleasure as his supreme good. The series of criminal amours in which he was almost incessantly engaged during this time, must probably have afforded some remarkable adventures and occurrences; but the memory of them has perished. Nor do I think it unworthy of notice here, that amidst all the intimacy of our friendship, and the many hours of cheerful as well as serious converse which we spent together, I never remember to have heard him speak of any of these intrigues, otherwise than in the general with deep and solemn abhorrence. This I the rather mention, as it seemed a most genuine proof of his unfeigned repentance, which I think there is great reason to suspect, when people seem to take a pleasure in relating and describing scenes of vicious indulgence, which they yet profess to have disapproved and forsaken.

Amidst all these pernicious wanderings from the paths of religion, virtue, and happiness, he approved himself so well in his military character, that he was made a lieutenant in that year, viz. 1706; and I am told he was very quickly after promoted to a cornet's commission in Lord Stair's regiment of the Scots Greys, and, on the 31st of January, 1714–15, was made captain-lieutenant in Colonel Ker's regiment of dragoons. He had the honour of being known to the Earl of Stair some time before, and was made his aid-de-camp; and when, upon his Lordship's being appointed ambassador from his late Majesty to the court of France, he made so splendid an entrance into Paris, Captain Gardiner was his master of the horse; and I have been told that a great deal of the care of that admirably well-adjusted ceremony fell upon him; so that he gained great credit by the manner in which he conducted it. Under the benign influence of his Lordship's favour, which to the last day of his life he retained, a captain's commission was procured for him, dated July 22, 1715, in the regiment of dragoons commanded by Colonel Stanhope, now Earl of Harrington; and in 1717 he was advanced to the majority of that regiment, in which office he continued till it was reduced on November 10, 1718, when he was put out of commission. But when his Majesty, king George I., was thoroughly apprised of his faithful and important services, he gave him his sign-manual, entitling him to the first majority that should become vacant in any regiment of horse or dragoons, which happened, about five years after, to be in Croft's regiment of dragoons, in which he received a commission, dated 1st June, 1724; and on the 20th of July the same year, he was made major of an older regiment, commanded by the Earl of Stair.

As I am now speaking of so many of his military preferments, I will dispatch the account of them by observing, that, on the 24th January 1729–30, he was advanced to the rank of lieutenant-colonel in the same regiment, long under the command of Lord Cadogan, with whose friendship this brave and vigilant officer was also honoured for many years. And he continued in this rank and regiment till the 19th of April, 1743, when he received a colonel's commission over a regiment of dragoons lately commanded by Brigadier Bland, at the head of which he valiantly fell, in the defence of his sovereign and his country, about two years and a half after he received it.

We will now return to that period of his life which was passed at Paris, the scene of such remarkable and important events. He continued (if I remember right) several years under the roof of the brave and generous Earl of Stair, to whom he endeavoured to approve himself by every instance of diligent and faithful service. And his Lordship gave no inconsiderable proof of the dependence which he had upon him, when, in the beginning of 1715, he entrusted him with the important dispatches relating to a discovery which, by a series of admirable policy, he had made of a design which the French king was then forming for invading Great Britain in favour of the Pretender; in which the French apprehended they were so sure of success, that it seemed a point of friendship in one of the chief counsellors of that court to dissuade a dependent of his from accepting some employment under his Britannic majesty, when proposed by his envoy there, because it was said that in less than six weeks there would be a revolution in favour of what they called the family of the Stuarts. The captain dispatched his journey with the utmost speed; a variety of circumstances happily concurred to accelerate it; and they who remember how soon the regiments which that emergency required, were raised and armed, will, I doubt not, esteem it a memorable instance, both of the most cordial zeal in the friends of the government, and of the gracious care of Divine Providence over the house of Hanover and the British liberties, so inseparably connected with its interest.

While Captain Gardiner was at London, in one of the journeys he made upon this occasion, he, with that frankness which was natural to him, and which in those days was not always under the most prudent restraint, ventured to predict, from what he knew of the bad state of the French king's health, that he would not live six weeks. This was made known by some spies who were at St. James's, and came to be reported at the court of Versailles; for he received letters from some friends at Paris, advising him not to return thither, unless he could reconcile himself to a lodging in the Bastile. But he was soon free from that apprehension; for, if I mistake not, before half that time was accomplished, Louis XIV. died, (Sept. 1, 1715,) and it is generally thought his death was hastened by a very accidental circumstance, which had some reference to the captain's prophecy; for the last time he ever dined in public, which was a very little while after the report of it had been made there, he happened to discover our British envoy among the spectators. The penetration of this illustrious person was too great, and his attachment to the interest of his royal master too well known, not to render him very disagreeable to that crafty and tyrannical prince, whom God had so long suffered to be the disgrace of monarchy, and the scourge of Europe. He at first appeared very languid, as indeed he was; but on casting his eye upon the Earl of Stair, he affected to appear before him in a much better state of health than he really was; and therefore, as if he had been awakened on a sudden from some deep reverie, he immediately put himself into an erect posture, called up a laboured vivacity into his countenance, and ate much more heartily than was by any means advisable, repeating two or three times to a nobleman, (I think the Duke of Bourbon) then in waiting, "*Il me semble que je ne mange pas mal pour un homme qui devoit mourir si tot.*" "Methinks I eat very well for a man who is to die so soon." But this inroad upon that regularity of living which he had for some time observed, agreed so ill with him that he never recovered this meal, but died in less than a fortnight. This gave occasion for some humorous people to say, that old Louis, after all, was killed by a Briton. But if this story be true, (which I think there can be no room to doubt, as the colonel, from whom I have often heard it, though absent, could scarce be misinformed,) it might more properly be said that he fell by his own vanity; in which view I thought it so remarkable, as not to be unworthy of a place in these memoirs.

The captain quickly returned, and continued, with small interruptions, at Paris, at least till

1720, and how much longer I do not certainly know. The Earl's favour and generosity made him easy in his affairs, though he was, (as has been observed before,) part of the time, out of commission, by breaking the regiment to which he belonged, of which before he was major. This was in all probability the gayest part of his life, and the most criminal. Whatever wise and good examples he might find in the family where he had the honour to reside, it is certain that the French court, during the regency of the Duke of Orleans, was one of the most dissolute under heaven. What, by a wretched abuse of language, have been called intrigues of love and gallantry, were so entirely to the major's then degenerate taste, that if not the whole business, at least the whole happiness of his life, consisted in them; and he had now too much leisure for one who was so prone to abuse it. His fine constitution, than which perhaps there was hardly ever a better, gave him great opportunities of indulging himself in these excesses; and his good spirits enabled him to pursue his pleasures of every kind in so alert and sprightly a manner, that multitudes envied him, and called him, by a dreadful kind of compliment, "the happy rake."

CHAPTER IV.

CHECKS OF CONSCIENCE.

Yet still the checks of conscience, and some remaining principles of so good an education, would break in upon his most licentious hours; and I particularly remember he told me, that when some of his dissolute companions were once congratulating him on his distinguished felicity, a dog happening at that time to come into the room, he could not forbear groaning inwardly, and saying to himself, 'Oh that I were that dog!' Such then was his happiness; and such perhaps is that of hundreds more who bear themselves highest in the contempt of religion, and glory in that infamous servitude which they affect to call liberty. But these remonstrances of reason and conscience were in vain; and, in short, he carried things so far in this wretched part of his life, that I am well assured some sober English gentlemen, who made no great pretences to religion, how agreeable soever he might have been to them on other accounts, rather declined than sought his company, as fearing they might have been ensnared and corrupted by it.

Yet I cannot find that in these most abandoned days he was fond of drinking. Indeed, he never had any natural relish for that kind of intemperance, from which he used to think a manly pride might be sufficient to preserve persons of sense and spirit; as by it they give up every thing that distinguishes them from the meanest of their species, or indeed from animals the most below it. So that if ever he fell into any excesses of this kind, it was merely out of complaisance to his company, and that he might not appear stiff and singular. His frank, obliging, and generous temper procured him many friends; and these principles, which rendered him amiable to others, not being under the direction of true wisdom and piety, sometimes made him, in the ways of living he pursued, more uneasy to himself than he might, perhaps, have been, if he could have entirely overcome them; especially as he never was a sceptic in his principles, but still retained a secret apprehension that natural and revealed religion, though he did not much care to think of either, were founded in truth. And, with this conviction, his notorious violations of the most essential precepts of both could not but occasion some secret misgivings of heart. His continual neglect of the great Author of his being, of whose perfections he could not doubt, and to whom he knew himself to be under daily and perpetual obligations, gave him, in some moments of involuntary reflection, inexpressible remorse; and this at times wrought upon him to such a degree, that he resolved he would attempt to pay him some acknowledgments. Accordingly, for a few mornings he did it, repeating in retirement some passages out of the Psalms, and perhaps other scriptures which he still retained in his memory; and owning, in a few strong words, the many mercies and deliverances he had received, and the ill returns he had made for them.

I find, among the other papers transmitted to me, the following verses, which I have heard him repeat, as what had impressed him a good deal in his unconverted state; and as I suppose they did something towards setting him on this effort towards devotion, and might probably furnish a part of these orisons, I hope I need make no apology to my reader for inserting them, especially as I do not recollect that I have seen them any where else.

Attend, my soul! the early birds inspire
My grovelling thoughts with pure celestial fire;
They from their temperate sleep awake, and pay
Their thankful anthems for the new-born day.
See how the tuneful lark is mounted high,
And, poet-like, salutes the eastern sky!
He warbles through the fragrant air his lays,
And seems the beauties of the morn to praise.
But man, more void of gratitude awakes,
And gives no thanks for the sweet rest he takes;
Looks on the glorious sun's new kindled flame,
Without one thought of Him from whom it came.
The wretch unhallowed does the day begin,
Shakes off his sleep, but shakes not off his sin.

But these strains were too devout to continue long in a heart as yet quite unsanctified; for how readily soever he could repeat such acknowledgments of the Divine power, presence, and goodness, and own his own follies and faults, he was stopped short by the remonstrances of conscience as to the flagrant absurdity of confessing sins he did not desire to forsake, and of pretending to praise God for his mercies, when he did not endeavour to live to his service, and to behave in such a manner as gratitude, if sincere, would plainly dictate. A model of devotion where such sentiments made no part, his good sense could not digest; and the use of such language before a heart-searching God, merely as an hypocritical form, while the sentiments of his soul were contrary to it, justly appeared to him such daring profaneness, that, irregular as the state of his mind was, the thought of it struck him with horror. He therefore determined to make no more attempts of this sort, and was perhaps one of the first who deliberately laid aside prayer from some sense of God's omniscience, and some natural principle of honour and conscience.

These secret debates with himself and ineffectual efforts would sometimes return; but they were overborne again and again by the force of temptation, and it is no wonder that in consequence of them his heart grew yet harder. Nor was it softened or awakened by some very memorable deliverances which at this time he received. He was in extreme danger by a fall from his horse, as he was riding post I think in the streets of Calais. When going down a hill, the horse threw him over his head, and pitched over him; so that when he rose, the beast lay beyond him, and almost dead. Yet, though he received not the least harm, it made no serious impression on his mind. On his return from England in the packet-boat, if I remember right, but a few weeks after the former accident, a violent storm, that drove them up to Harwich, tossed them from thence for several hours in a dark night on the coast of Holland, and brought them into such extremity, that the captain of the vessel urged him to go to prayers immediately, if he ever intended to do it at all; for he concluded they would in a few minutes be at the bottom of the sea. In this circumstance he did pray, and that very fervently too; and it was very remarkable, that while he was crying to God for deliverance, the wind fell, and quickly after they arrived at Calais. But the major was so little affected with what had befallen him, that when some of his gay friends, on hearing the story, rallied him upon the efficacy of his prayers, he excused himself from the scandal of being thought much in earnest, by saying "that it was at midnight, an hour when his good mother and aunt were asleep, or else he should have left that part of the business to them;"—a speech which I should not have mentioned, but as it shows in so lively a view the wretched situation of his mind at that time, though his great deliverance from the power of darkness was then nearly approaching. He recounted these things to me with the greatest humility, as showing how utterly unworthy he was of that miracle of divine grace by which he was quickly after brought to so true and so permanent a sense of religion.

CHAPTER V.

HIS CONVERSION.

AND now I am come to that astonishing part of his story, the account of his conversion, which I cannot enter upon without assuring the reader that I have sometimes been tempted to suppress many circumstances of it; not only as they may seem incredible to some, and enthusiastical to others, but I am very sensible they are liable to great abuses; which was the reason that he gave me for concealing the most extraordinary from many persons to whom he mentioned some of the rest. And I believe it was this, together with the desire of avoiding every thing that might look like ostentation on this head, that prevented his leaving a written account of it, though I have often entreated him to do it, as I particularly remember I did in the very last letter I ever wrote him, and pleaded the possibility of his falling amidst those dangers to which I knew his valour might, in such circumstances, naturally expose him. I was not so happy as to receive any answer to this letter, which reached him but a few days before his death; nor can I certainly say whether he had or had not complied with my request, as it is very possible a paper of this kind, if it were written, might be lost amidst the ravages which the rebels made when they plundered Bankton.

The story, however, was so remarkable, that I had little reason to apprehend I should ever forget it; and yet, to guard against all contingencies of that kind, I wrote it down that very evening, as I heard it from his own mouth; and I have now before me the memoirs of that conversation, dated Aug. 14, 1739, which conclude with these words, (which I added that if we should both have died that night, the world might not have lost this edifying and affecting history, or have wanted any attestation of it I was capable of giving): "N. B. I have written down this account with all the exactness I am capable of, and could safely take an oath of it as to the truth of every circumstance, to the best of my remembrance, as the colonel related it to me a few hours ago." I do not know that I had reviewed this paper since I wrote it, till I set myself thus publicly to record this extraordinary fact; but I find it punctually to agree with what I have often related from my memory, which I charged carefully with so wonderful and important a fact. It is with all solemnity that I now deliver it down to posterity as in the sight and presence of God; and I choose deliberately to expose myself to those severe censures which the haughty but empty scorn of infidelity, or princicles nearly approaching it, and effectually doing its pernicious work, may very probably dictate upon the occasion, rather than to smother a relation, which may, in the judgment of my conscience, be like to conduce so much to the glory of God, the honour of the gospel, and the good of mankind. One thing more I will only premise, that I hope none who have heard the colonel himself speak something of this wonderful scene, will be surprised if they find some new circumstances here; because he assured me, at the time he first gave me the whole narration, (which was in the very room in which I now write,) that he had never imparted it so fully to any living before; yet, at the same time, he gave me full liberty to communicate it to whomsoever I should in my conscience judge it might be useful to do it, whether before or after his death. Accordingly I did, while he was alive, recount almost every circumstance I am now going to write, to several pious friends; referring them at the same time to the colonel himself, whenever they might have an opportunity of seeing or writing to him, for a further confirmation of what I told them, if they judged it requisite. They *glorified God in him;* and I humbly hope many of my readers will also do it. They will soon perceive the reason of so much caution in my introduction to this story, for which, therefore, I shall make no further apology.*

This memorable event happened towards the middle of July, 1719; but I cannot be exact as to the day. The major had spent the evening (and if I mistake not, it was the Sabbath) in some gay company, and had an unhappy assig-

*It is no small satisfaction to me, since I wrote this, to have received a letter from the Rev. Mr. Spears, minister of the gospel at Burntisland, dated Jan. 14, 1746–7, in which he relates to me this whole story, as he had it from the colonel's own mouth about four years after he gave me the narration. There is not a single circumstance in which either of our narrations disagrees; and every one of the particulars in mine, which seems most astonishing, is attested by this, and sometimes in stronger words, one only ex cepted, on which I shall add a short remark when I come to it. As this letter was written near Lady Frances Gardiner at her desire, and attended with a postscript from her own hand, this is, in effect, a sufficient attestation how agreeable it was to those accounts which she must often have heard the colonel give of this matter.

nation with a married woman, of what rank or quality I did not particularly inquire, whom he was to attend exactly at twelve. The company broke up about eleven; and not judging it convenient to anticipate the time appointed, he went into his chamber to kill the tedious hour, perhaps with some amusing book, or in some other way. But it very accidentally happened that he took up a religious book which his good mother or aunt had, without his knowledge, slipped into his portmanteau. It was called, if I remember the title exactly, *The Christian Soldier, or Heaven taken by Storm,* and was written by Mr. Thomas Watson. Guessing by the title of it that he should find some phrases of his own profession spiritualized in a manner which he thought might afford him some diversion, he resolved to dip into it; but he took no serious notice of any thing he read in it; and yet, while this book was in his hand, an impression was made upon his mind, (perhaps God only knows how,) which drew after it a train of the most important and happy consequences.

There is indeed a possibility, that while he was sitting in this solitude, and reading in this careless and profane manner, he might suddenly fall asleep, and only dream of what he apprehended he saw. But nothing can be more certain than that, when he gave me this relation, he judged himself to have been as broad awake during the whole time as he ever was in any part of his life; and he mentioned it to me several times afterwards as what undoubtedly passed, not only in his imagination, but before his eyes.*

He thought he saw an unusual blaze of light fall on the book while he was reading, which he at first imagined might happen by some accident in the candle. But, lifting up his eyes, he apprehended, to his extreme amazement, that there was before him, as it were suspended in the air, a visible representation of the Lord Jesus Christ upon the cross, surrounded on all sides with a glory; and was impressed as if a voice, or something equivalent to a voice, had come to him to this effect, (for he was not confident as to the

* Mr. Spears, in the letter mentioned above, where he introduces the colonel telling his own story, has these words: "All of a sudden there was presented in a very lively manner to my view, or to my mind, a representation of my glorious Redeemer," &c. And this gentleman adds, in a parenthesis, "It was so lively and striking, that he could not tell whether it was to his bodily eyes, or to those of his mind." This makes me think that what I had said to him on the phenomena of visions, apparitions, &c., (as being, when most real, supernatural impressions on the imagination, rather than attended with any external object,) had some influence upon him. Yet still it is evident he looked upon this as a vision, whether it was before the eyes or in the mind, and not as a dream.

very words,) "Oh, sinner! did I suffer this for thee, and are these the returns?" But whether this were an audible voice, or only a strong impression on his mind equally striking, he did not seem very confident, though, to the best of my remembrance, he rather judged it to be the former. Struck with so amazing a phenomenon as this, there remained hardly any life in him, so that he sunk down in the arm-chair in which he sat, and continued, he knew not exactly how long, insensible; (which was one circumstance that made me several times take the liberty to suggest that he might possibly be all this while asleep;) but however that were, he quickly after opened his eyes, and saw nothing more than usual.

It may easily be supposed he was in no condition to make any observations upon the time in which he had remained in an insensible state; nor did he, throughout all the remainder of the night, once recollect that criminal and detestable assignation which had before engrossed all his thoughts. He rose in a tumult of passions not to be conceived, and walked to and fro in his chamber till he was ready to drop down in unutterable astonishment and agony of heart, appearing to himself the vilest monster in the creation of God, who had all his lifetime been crucifying Christ afresh by his sins, and now saw, as he assuredly believed, by a miraculous vision, the horror of what he had done. With this was connected such a view of both the majesty and goodness of God, as caused him to loathe and abhor himself, and to repent as in dust and ashes. He immediately gave judgment against himself, that he was most justly worthy of eternal damnation; he was astonished that he had not been immediately struck dead in the midst of his wickedness; and (which I think deserves particular remark) though he assuredly believed that he should ere long be in hell, and settled it as a point with himself for several months that the wisdom and justice of God did almost necessarily require that such an enormous sinner should be made an example of everlasting vengeance, and a spectacle as such both to angels and men, so that he hardly durst presume to pray for pardon; yet what he then suffered was not so much from the fear of hell, though he concluded it would soon be his portion, as from a sense of that horrible ingratitude he had shown to the God of his life, and to that blessed Redeemer who had been in so affecting a manner set forth as crucified before him.

To this he refers in a letter dated from Douglas, the 1st of April 1725, communicated to me by his lady,* but I know not to whom it was addressed. His words are these: "One thing relating to my conversion, and a remarkable instance of the goodness of God to me, *the chief of sinners*, I do not remember that I ever told to any other person. It was this, that after the astonishing sight I had of my blessed Lord, the terrible condition in which I was proceeded not so much from the terrors of the law, as from a sense of having been so ungrateful a monster to him whom I thought I saw pierced for my transgressions." I the rather insert these words, as they evidently attest the circumstance which

* Where I make any extracts as from Colonel Gardiner's letters, they are either from originals, which I have in my own hands, or from copies which were transmitted to me from persons of undoubted credit, chiefly by the Right Honourable the Lady Frances Gardiner, through the hands of the Rev. Mr. Webster, one of the ministers of Edinburgh. This I the rather mention, because some letters have been brought to me as Colonel Gardiner's, concerning which I have not only been very dubious, but morally certain that they could not have been written by him. I have also heard of many who have been fond of assuring the world that they were well acquainted with him, and were near him when he fell, whose reports have been most inconsistent with each other, as well as contrary to that testimony relating to the circumstances of his death, which, on the whole, appeared to me beyond controversy the most natural and authentic; from whence, therefore, I shall take my account of that affecting scene.

may seem most amazing in this affair, and contain so express a declaration of his own apprehension concerning it.

In this view it may naturally be supposed that he passed the remainder of the night waking, and he could get but little rest in several that followed. His mind was continually taken up in reflecting on the divine purity and goodness; the grace which had been proposed to him in the gospel, and which he had rejected; the singular advantages he had enjoyed and abused; and the many favours of providence which he had received, particularly in rescuing him from so many imminent dangers of death, which he now saw must have been attended with such dreadful and hopeless destruction. The privileges of his education, which he had so much despised, now lay with an almost insupportable weight on his mind; and the folly of that career of sinful pleasure which he had so many years been running with desperate eagerness and unworthy delight, now filled him with indignation against himself, and against the great deceiver, by whom (to use his own phrase) he had been "so wretchedly and scandalously befooled." This he used often to express in the strongest terms, which I shall not repeat so particularly, as I cannot recollect some of them. But on the whole it is certain that, by what passed before he left his chamber the next day, the whole frame and disposition of his soul was new-modelled and changed; so that he became, and continued to the last day of his exemplary and truly Christian life, the very reverse of what he had been before. A variety of particulars, which I am afterwards to mention, will illustrate this in the most convincing manner. But I cannot proceed to them without pausing to adore so illustrious an instance of the power and freedom of divine grace, and entreating my reader seriously to reflect upon it, that his own heart may be suitably affected. For surely, if the truth of the fact be admitted in the lowest views in which it can be placed, (that is, supposing the first impression to have passed in a dream,) it must be allowed to have been little, if anything less than miraculous. It cannot in the course of nature be imagined how such a dream should arise in a mind full of the most impure ideas and affections, and (as he himself often pleaded) more alienated from the thoughts of a crucified Saviour, than from any other object that can be conceived; nor can we surely suppose it should, without a mighty energy of the divine power, be effectual to produce not only some transient flow of passion, but so entire and permanent a change in character and conduct.

On the whole, therefore, I must beg leave to express my own sentiments of the matter, by repeating on this occasion what I wrote several years ago, in my eighth sermon on regeneration, in a passage dictated chiefly by the circumstantial knowledge which I had of this amazing story, and methinks sufficiently vindicated by it, if it stood entirely alone, which yet, I must take the liberty to say, it does not; for I hope the world will be particularly informed, that there is at least a second that very nearly approaches it, whenever the established church of England shall lose one of its brightest living ornaments, and one of the most useful members which that, or perhaps any other Christian communion, can boast. In the mean time, may his exemplary life be long continued, and his zealous ministry abundantly prospered! I beg my reader's pardon for this digression. The passage I referred to above is remarkably, though not equally, applicable to both the cases, under that head where I am showing that God sometimes accomplishes the great work of which we speak, by secret and immediate impressions on the mind. After preceding illustrations, there are the following words, on which the colonel's conversion will throw the justest light. "Yea, I have known those of distinguished genius, polite manners, and great experience in human affairs, who, after having out-grown all the impressions of a religious education—after having been hardened, rather than subdued by the most singular mercies, even various, repeated, and astonishing deliverances, which have appeared to themselves as no less than miraculous—after having lived for years without God in the world, notoriously corrupt themselves, and labouring to the utmost to corrupt others, have been stopped on a sudden in the full career of their sin, and have felt such rays of the divine presence, and of redeeming love, darting in upon their minds, almost like lightning from heaven, as have at once roused, overpowered, and transformed them; so that they have come out of their secret chambers with an irreconcilable enmity to those vices to which, when they entered them, they were the tamest and most abandoned slaves; and have appeared from that very hour the votaries, the patrons, the champions of religion; and after a course of the most resolute attachment to it, in spite of all the reasonings or the railleries, the importunities or the reproaches of its enemies, they have continued to this day some of its brightest ornaments; a change which I behold with equal wonder and delight, and which, if a nation should join in deriding it, I would adore as the finger of God."

The mind of Major Gardiner continued from this remarkable time, till towards the end of October, (that is rather more than three months, but especially the first two of them,) in as extraordinary a situation as one can well imagine. He knew nothing of the joys arising from a sense of pardon; but, on the contrary, for the greater part of that time, and with very short intervals of hope towards the end of it, took it for granted that he must in all probability quickly perish. Nevertheless, he had such a sense of the evil of sin, of the goodness of the Divine Being, and of the admirable tendency of the Christian revelation, that he resolved to spend the remainder of his life, while God continued him out of hell, in as rational and as useful a manner as he could; and to continue casting himself at the foot of divine mercy every day, and often in a day, if peradventure there might be hope of pardon, of which all that he could say was, that he did not absolutely despair. He had at that time such a sense of the degeneracy of his own heart, that he hardly durst form any determinate resolution against sin, or pretend to engage himself by any vow in the presence of God; but he was continually crying to him, that he would deliver him from the bondage of corruption. He perceived in himself a most surprising alteration with regard to the dispositions of his heart; so that, though he felt little of the delight of religious duties, he extremely desired opportunities of being engaged in them; and those licentious pleasures which had before been his heaven, were now absolutely his aversion. And indeed, when I consider how habitual all those criminal indulgences were grown to him, and that he was now in the prime of life, and all this while in high health too, I cannot but be astonished to reflect upon it, that he should be so wonderfully sanctified in body, as well as in soul and spirit, as that, for all the future years of his life, he from that hour should find so constant a disinclination to, and abhorrence of, those criminal sensualities to which he fancied he was before so invincibly impelled by his very constitution, that he was used strangely to think, and to say, that Omnipotence itself could not reform him, without destroying that body, and giving him another.*

Nor was he only delivered from that bondage of corruption which had been habitual to

* Mr. Spears expresses this wonderful circumstance in these remarkable words: "I was (said the colonel to me) effectually cured of all inclination to that sin I was so strongly addicted to, that I thought nothing but shooting me through the head could have cured me of it; and all desire and inclination to it was removed, as entirely as if I had been a sucking child; nor did the temptation return to this day." Mr. Webster's words on the same subject are these: "One thing I have heard the colonel frequently say, that he was much addicted to impurity before his acquaintance with religion; but that, so soon as he was enlightened from above, he *felt the power of the Holy Ghost* changing his nature so wonderfully, that his sanctification in this respect seemed more remarkable than in any other." On which that worthy person makes this very reasonable reflection: "So thorough a change of such a polluted nature, evidenced by the most unblemished walk and conversation for a long course of years, demonstrates indeed the power of the Highest, and leaves no room to doubt of its reality." Mr. Spears says, this happened in three days' time; but from what I can recollect, all that the colonel could mean by that expression, if he used it, (as I conclude he did,) was that he began to make the observation in the space of three days: whereas, during that time, his thoughts were so taken up with the wonderful views presented to his mind, that he did not immediately attend to it. If he had, within the first three days, any temptation to seek some ease from the anguish of his mind, in returning to former sensualities, it is a circumstance he did not mention to me; and by what I can recollect of the strain of his discourse, he intimated if he did not express the contrary.

him for many years, but felt in his breast so contrary a disposition, that he was grieved to see human nature, in those to whom he was most entirely a stranger, prostituted to such low and contemptible pursuits. He therefore exerted his natural courage in a very new kind of combat, and became an open advocate for religion in all its principles, so far as he was acquainted with them, and all its precepts, relating to sobriety, righteousness, and godliness. Yet he was very desirous and cautious that he might not run into extremes, and made it one of his first petitions to God, the very day after these amazing impressions had been wrought in his mind, that he might not be suffered to behave with such an affected strictness and preciseness as would lead others about him into mistaken notions of religion, and expose it to reproach or suspicion, as if it were an unlovely or uncomfortable thing. For this reason, he endeavoured to appear as cheerful in conversation as he conscientiously could; though, in spite of all his precautions, some traces of that deep inward sense which he had of his guilt and misery would at times appear. He made no secret of it, however, that his views were entirely changed, though he concealed the particular circumstances attending that change. He told his most intimate companions freely that he had reflected on the course of life in which he had so long joined them, and found it to be folly and madness, unworthy a rational creature, and much more unworthy persons calling themselves Christians. And he set up his standard, upon all occasions, against principles of infidelity and practices of vice, as determinately and as boldly as ever he displayed or planted his colours, when he bore them with so much honour in the field.

I cannot forbear mentioning one struggle of this kind which he described to me, with a large detail of circumstances, the first day of our acquaintance. There was at that time in Paris a certain lady (whose name, then well known in the grand and gay world, I must beg leave to conceal) who had imbibed the principles of deism, and valued herself much upon being an avowed advocate for them. The major, with his usual frankness, (though I doubt not with that politeness of manners which was so habitual to him, and which he retained throughout his whole life,) answered her like a man who perfectly saw through the fallacy of her arguments, and was grieved to the heart for her delusions. On this she briskly challenged him to debate the matter at large, and to fix upon a day for that purpose, when he should dine with her, attended by any clergyman he might choose, whether of the Protestant or Catholic communion. A sense of duty would not allow him to decline this challenge; and yet he had no sooner accepted it, but he was thrown into great perplexity and distress lest, being, as I remember he expressed it when he told me the story, only a Christian of six weeks old, he should prejudice so good a cause by his unskilful manner of defending it. However, he sought his refuge in earnest and repeated prayers to God, that he who can ordain strength, and perfect praise, out of the mouth of babes and sucklings, would graciously enable him on this occasion to vindicate his truths in a manner which might carry conviction along with it. He then endeavoured to marshal the arguments in his own mind as well as he could; and apprehending that he could not speak with so much freedom before a number of persons, especially before such whose province he might seem in that case to invade, if he had not devolved the principal part of the discourse upon them, he easily admitted the apology of a clergyman or two, to whom he mentioned the affair, and waited on the lady alone upon the day appointed. But his heart was so set upon the business, that he came earlier than he was expected, and time enough to have two hours' discourse before dinner; nor did he at all decline having two persons, nearly related to the lady, present during the conference. The major opened it, with a view of such arguments for the Christian religion as he had digested in his own mind, to prove that the apostles were not mistaken themselves, and that they could not have intended to impose upon us, in the accounts they give of the grand facts they attest; with the truth of which facts, that of the Christian religion is most apparently connected. And it was a great encouragement to him to find, that unaccustomed as he was to discourses of this nature, he had an unusual command both of thought and expression, so that he recollected and uttered every thing as he could have wished. The lady heard with attention; and though he paused between every branch of the argument, she did not interrupt the course of it till he told her he had finished his design, and waited for her reply. She then produced some of her objections, which he took up and canvassed in such a manner that at length she burst into tears, allowed the force of his arguments and replies, and appeared for some time after so deeply impressed with the conversation, that it was observed by several of her friends; and there is reason to believe that the impression continued, at least so far as to prevent her from ever appearing under the character of an unbeliever or a sceptic.

This is only one specimen among many of the battles he was almost daily called out to fight in the cause of religion and virtue; with relation to which I find him expressing himself thus in a letter to Mrs. Gardiner, his good mother, dated from Paris the 25th of January following, that is 1719-20, in answer to one in which she had warned him to expect such trials: "I have (says he) already met with them, and am obliged to fight, and to dispute every inch of ground. But all thanks and praise to the great Captain of my salvation. He fights for me, and then it is no wonder that I come off more than conqueror:" by which last expression I suppose he meant to insinuate that he was strengthened and established, rather than overborne, by this opposition. Yet it was not immediately that he gained such fortitude. He has often told me how much he felt in those days of the emphasis of those well-chosen words of the apostle, in which he ranks the trial of cruel mockings, with scourgings, and bonds, and imprisonments. The continual railleries with which he was received, in almost all companies where he had been most familiar before, did often distress him beyond measure; so that he several times declared he would much rather have marched up to a battery of the enemy's cannon, than have been obliged, so continually as he was, to face such artillery as this. But, like a brave soldier in the first action wherein he is engaged, he continued resolute, though shuddering at the terror of the assault; and quickly overcame those impressions which it is not perhaps in nature wholly to avoid; and therefore I find him, in the letter above referred to, which was written about half a year after his conversion, "quite ashamed to think of the uneasiness which these things once gave him." In a word, he went on, as every resolute Christian by divine grace may do, till he turned ridicule and opposition into respect and veneration.

But this sensible triumph over these difficulties was not till his Christian experience had been abundantly advanced by the blessing of God on the sermons he heard, (particularly in the Swiss chapel,) and on the many hours which he spent in devout retirement, pouring out his whole soul before God in prayer. He began, within about two months after his first memorable change, to perceive some secret dawnings of more cheerful hope, that vile as he saw himself to be, (and I believe no words can express how vile that was,) he might nevertheless obtain mercy through the Redeemer. At length (if I remember right, about the end of October, 1719) he found all the burthen of his mind taken off at once by the powerful impression of that memorable scripture on his mind, Romans iii. 25, 26, "Whom God hath set forth for a propitiation through faith in his blood, to declare his righteousness in the remission of sins,—that he might be just, and the justifier of him that believeth in Jesus." He had used to imagine that the justice of God required the damnation of so enormous a sinner as he saw himself to be; but now he was made deeply sensible that the divine justice might be not only vindicated, but glorified, in saving him by the blood of Jesus, even that blood which cleanseth us from all sin. Then did he see and feel the riches of redeeming love and grace in such a manner as not only engaged him with the utmost pleasure and confidence to venture his soul upon it, but even swallowed up, as it were, his whole heart in the returns of love, which from that blessed time became the genuine and delightful principle of his obedience, and animated him, with an enlarged heart, to run the way of God's commandments. Thus God was pleased (as he himself used to speak) in an hour to turn his captivity. All the terrors of his former state were changed into unutterable joy, which kept him almost continually waking for three nights together, and yet refreshed him as the noblest of cordials. His expressions, though naturally very strong, always seemed to be swallowed up when he would describe the series of thought through which he now passed, under the rapturous experience of that joy unspeakable and full of glory, which then seemed to overflow his very soul, as indeed there was nothing he seemed to speak of with greater relish. And though the first ecstacies of it afterwards subsided into a more calm and composed delight, yet were the impressions so deep and so permanent, that he assured me, on the word of a Christian and a friend, wonderful as it might seem, that, for about seven years after this, he enjoyed almost heaven upon earth. His soul was so continually filled with a sense of the love of God in Christ, that it knew little interruption, but when necessary converse, and the duties of his station, called off his thoughts for a little time. And when they did so, as soon as he was alone, the torrent returned into its natural channel again; so that, from the minute of awakening in the morning, his heart was raised to God, and triumphing in him; and these thoughts attended him through all the scenes of life, till he lay down on his bed again, and a short parenthesis of sleep (for it was but a very short one that he allowed himself) invigorated his animal powers, for renewing them with greater intenseness and sensibility.

I shall have an opportunity of illustrating this in the most convincing manner below, by extracts from several letters which he wrote to intimate friends during this happy period of time—letters which breathe a spirit of such sublime and fervent piety as I have seldom met with any where else. In these circumstances, it is no wonder that he was greatly delighted with Dr. Watts's imitation of the 126th Psalm, since it may be questioned whether there ever was a person to whom the following stanzas of it were more suitable :—

When God revealed his gracious name,
  And changed my mournful state,
My rapture seemed a pleasing dream;
  Thy grace appeared so great.

The world beheld the glorious change,
  And did thine hand confess;
My tongue broke out in unknown strains,
  And sung surprising grace.

"Great is the work," my neighbours cried,
  And owned the power divine:
"Great is the work," my heart replied,
  "And be the glory thine."

The Lord can change the darkest skies,
  Can give us day for night,
Make drops of sacred sorrow rise,
  To rivers of delight.

Let those that sow in sadness, wait
  Till the fair harvest come!
They shall confess their sheaves are great.
  And shout the blessings home.

I have been so happy as to get the sight of five original letters which he wrote to his mother about this time, which do, in a very lively manner, illustrate the surprising change made in the whole current of his thoughts and temper of his mind. Many of them were written in the most hasty manner, just as the courier who brought them was perhaps unexpectedly setting out, and they relate chiefly to affairs in which the public is not at all concerned; yet there is not one of them in which he has not inserted some warm and genuine sentiment of religion. Indeed it is very remarkable, that though he was pleased to honour me with a great many letters, and I have seen several more which he wrote to others, some of them on journeys, where he could have but a few minutes at command, yet I cannot recollect that I ever saw any one in which there was not some trace of piety; and the Rev. Mr. Webster, who was employed to review great numbers of them, that he might select such extracts as he should think proper to communicate to me, has made the same observation.*

The major, with great justice, tells the good lady his mother, "that when she saw him again she would find the person indeed the same, but every thing else entirely changed." And she

* His words are these: "I have read over a vast number of the colonel's letters, and have not found any one of them, however short, and writ in the most passing manner, even when posting, but what is expressive of the most passionate breathings towards his God and Saviour. If the letter consists but of two sentences, religion is not forgot, which doubtless deserves to be carefully remarked, as the most uncontested evidence of a pious mind, ever under the warmest impressions of divine things."

might easily have perceived it of herself by the whole tenor of these letters, which every where breathe the unaffected spirit of a true Christian. They are taken up sometimes with giving advice and directions concerning some pious and charitable contributions, one of which, I remember, amounted to ten guineas, though as he was then out of commission, and had not formerly been very frugal, it cannot be supposed he had much to spare; sometimes in speaking of the pleasure with which he attended sermons, and expected sacramental opportunities; and at other times in exhorting her, established as she was in religion, to labour after a yet more exemplary character and conduct, or in recommending her to the divine presence and blessing, as well as himself to her prayers. What satisfaction such letters as these must give to a lady of her distinguished piety, who had so long wept over this dear and amiable son as quite lost to God, and on the verge of final destruction, it is not for me to describe, nor indeed to conceive. But hastily as these letters were written, only for private view, I will give a few specimens from them in his own words, which will serve to illustrate as well as confirm what I have hinted above.

"I must take the liberty," says he, in a letter

dated on the first day of the new year, or, according to the old style, Dec. 21, 1719, "to entreat you that you would receive no company on the Lord's day. I know you have a great many good acquaintance, with whose discourses one might be very well edified; but as you cannot keep out and let in whom you please, the best way, in my humble opinion, will be to see none." In another, of Jan. 25, "I am happier than any one can imagine, except I could put him exactly in the same situation with myself; which is what the world cannot give, and no man ever attained it, unless it were from above." In another, dated March 30, which was just before a sacrament day, "To-morrow, if it please God, I shall be happy, my soul being to be fed with the bread of life which came down from heaven. I shall be mindful of you all there." In another of Jan. 29, he thus expresses that indifference for worldly possessions which he so remarkably carried through the remainder of his life: "I know the rich are only stewards for the poor, and must give an account of every penny; therefore, the less I have, the more easy will it be to give an account of it." And to add no more from these letters at present, in the conclusion of one of them he has these comprehensive and solemn words: "Now that He, who is the ease of the afflicted, the support of the weak, the wealth of the poor, the teacher of the ignorant, the anchor of the fearful, and the infinite reward of all faithful souls, may pour out upon you all his richest blessings, shall always be the prayer of him who is entirely yours," &c.

To this account of his correspondence with his excellent mother, I should be glad to add a large view of another, to which she introduced him, with that reverend and valuable person under whose pastoral care she was placed—I mean the justly celebrated Doctor Edmund Calamy, to whom she could not but early communicate the joyful news of her son's conversion. I am not so happy as to be possessed of the letters which passed between them, which I have reason to believe would make a curious and valuable collection; but I have had the pleasure of receiving from my worthy and amiable friend, the Rev. Mr. Edmund Calamy, one of the letters the doctor, his father, wrote to the major on this wonderful occasion. I perceive by the contents of it that it was the first, and, indeed, it is dated as early as the 3d of August, 1719, which must be but a few days after his own account, dated August 4, N. S., could reach England. There is so much true religion and good sense in this paper, and the counsel it suggests may be so seasonable to other persons in circumstances which bear any resemblance to his, that I make no apology to my reader for inserting a large extract from it.

"DEAR SIR,—I conceive it will not much surprise you to understand that your good mother communicated to me your letter to her, dated August 4, N. S., which brought her the news you conceive would be so acceptable to her. I, who have often been a witness to her concern for you on a spiritual account, can attest with what joy this news was received by her, and imparted to me as a special friend, who she knew would bear a part with her on such an occasion. And, indeed, if (as our Saviour intimates, Luke xv. 7, 10,) there is, in such cases, joy in heaven and among the angels of God, it may be well supposed that of a pious mother who has spent so many prayers and tears upon you, and has, as it were, travailed in birth with you again till Christ was formed in you, could not be small. You may believe me if I add, that I also, as a common friend of hers and yours, and which is much more, of the Prince of Light, whom you now declare you heartily fall in with in opposition to that of the dark kingdom, could not but be tenderly affected with an account of it under your own hand. My joy on this account was the greater, considering the importance of your capacity, interests, and prospects, which, in such an age as this, may promise most happy consequences, on your heartily appearing on God's side, and embarking in the interest of our Redeemer. If I have hitherto at all remembered you at the throne of grace, at your good mother's desire, (which you are pleased to take notice of with so much respect,) I can assure you I shall henceforth be led to do it with more concern and particularity both by duty and inclination; and if I were capable of giving you any little assistance in the noble design you are engaging in, by corresponding with you by letter while you are at such a distance, I should do it most cheerfully. And perhaps such a motion may not be altogether unacceptable; for I am inclinable to believe, that when some whom you are obliged to converse with, observe your behaviour so different from what it formerly was, and banter you upon it as mad and fanciful, it may be some little relief to correspond with one who will take a pleasure in heartening and encouraging you. And when a great many things frequently offer, in which conscience may be concerned where duty may not always be plain, nor suitable persons to advise with at hand, it may be some satisfaction to you to correspond with one with whom you may use a friendly freedom in all such matters, and on whose fidelity you may depend. You may, therefore, command me in any of these respects, and I shall take a pleasure in serving you. One piece of advice I shall venture to give you, though your own good sense will make my enlarging upon it less needful—I mean, that you would, from your first setting out, carefully distinguish between the essentials of real religion, and those things which are commonly reckoned by its professors to belong to it. The want of this distinction has had very unhappy consequences from one age to another, and perhaps in none more than the present. But your daily converse with your Bible, which you mention, may herein give you great assistance. I move also, that since infidelity so much abounds, you would not only, by close and serious consideration, endeavour to settle yourself well in the fundamental principles of religion; but also that, as opportunity offers, you would converse with those books which treat most judiciously on the divine original of Christianity, such as Grotius, Abbadie, Baxter, Bates, Du Plessis, &c., which may establish you against the cavils that occur in almost all conversations, and furnish you with arguments which, when properly offered, may be of use to make some impression on others. But being too much straitened to enlarge at present, I can only add, that if your hearty falling in with serious religion should prove any hinderance to your advancement in the world, (which I pray God it may not, unless such advancement would be a real snare to you,) I hope you will trust our Saviour's word, that it shall be no disadvantage to you in the final issue: he has given you his word for it, Matt. xix. 29, upon which you may safely depend; and I am satisfied none that ever did so at last repented of it. May you go on and prosper, and the God of all grace and peace be with you!"

I think it very evident from the contents of this letter, that the major had not imparted to his mother the most singular circumstances attending his conversion; and indeed there was something so peculiar in them, that I do not wonder he was always cautious in speaking of them, and especially that he was at first much on the reserve. We may also naturally reflect that there seems to have been something very providential in this letter, considering the debate in which our illustrious convert was so soon engaged; for it was written but about three weeks before his conference with the lady above mentioned in the defence of Christianity, or at least before the appointment of it. And as some of the books recommended by Dr. Calamy, particularly Abbadie and Du Plessis, were undoubtedly within his reach, (if our English advocates were not,) this might, by the divine blessing, contribute considerably towards arming him for that combat in which he came off with such happy success. As in this instance, so in many others, they who will observe the coincidence and concurrence of things, may be engaged to adore the wise conduct of Providence in events which, when taken singly and by themselves, have nothing very remarkable in them.

I think it was about this time that this resolute and exemplary Christian entered upon that methodical manner of living which he pursued through so many succeeding years of life, and I believe generally, so far as the broken state of his health would allow it in his latter days, to the very end of it. He used constantly to rise at four in the morning, and to spend his time till six in the secret exercises of devotion, reading, meditation, and prayer, in which last he contracted such a fervency of spirit as I believe few men living ever obtained. This certainly tended very much to strengthen that firm faith in God, and reverent animating sense of his presence, for which he was so eminently remarkable, and which carried him through the trials and services of life with such steadiness and with such activity; for he indeed endured and acted as always seeing Him who is invisible. If at any time he was obliged to go out before six in the morning, he rose proportionably sooner; so that when a journey or a march has required him to be on horseback by four, he would be at his devotions at furthest by two. He likewise secured time for retirement in an evening; and that he might have it the more at command, and be the more fit to use it properly, as well as be better able to rise early the next morning, he generally went to bed about ten; and, during the time I was acquainted with him, he seldom ate any supper but a mouthful of bread, with one glass of wine. In consequence of this, as well as of his admirably good constitution, and the long habit he had formed, he required less sleep than most persons I have known; and I doubt not but his uncommon progress in piety was in a great measure owing to these resolute habits of self-denial.

A life anything like this could not, to be sure, be entered upon in the midst of such company as he had been accustomed to keep, without great opposition, especially as he did not entirely withdraw himself from all the circle of cheerful conversation; but, on the contrary, gave several hours every day to it, lest religion should be reproached as having made him morose. He however, early began a practice, which to the last day of his life he retained, of reproving vice and profaneness; and was never afraid to debate the matter with any one, under the consciousness of great superiority in the goodness of his cause.

A remarkable instance of this happened, if I mistake not, about the middle of 1720, though I cannot be very exact as to the date of the story. It was, however, on his first return to make any considerable abode in England after this remarkable change. He had heard, on the other side of the water, that it was currently reported among his companions at home that he was stark mad—a report at which no reader who knows the wisdom of the world in these matters, will be much surprised, any more than himself. He concluded, therefore, that he should have many battles to fight, and was willing to dispatch the business as fast as he could. And therefore, being to spend a few days at the country-house of a person of distinguished rank, with whom he had been very intimate, (whose name I do not remember that he told me, nor did I think it proper to inquire after it,) he begged the favour of him that he would contrive matters so, that, a day or two after he came down, several of their former gay companions might meet at his lordship's table, that he might have an opportunity of making his apology to them, and acquainting them with the nature and reasons of his change. It was accordingly agreed to; and a pretty large company met on the day appointed, with previous notice that Major Gardiner would be there. A good deal of raillery passed at dinner, to which the major made very little answer. But when the cloth was taken away, and the servants retired, he begged their patience for a few minutes, and then plainly and seriously told them what notions he entertained of virtue and religion, and on what considerations he had absolutely determined that by the grace of God he would make it the care and business of life, whatever he might lose by it, and whatever censure and contempt he might incur. He well knew how improper it was in such company to relate the extraordinary manner in which he was awakened, which they would probably have interpreted as a demonstration of lunacy, against all the gravity and solidity of his discourse; but he contented himself with such a rational defence of a righteous, sober, and godly life, as he knew none of them could with any shadow of reason contest. He then challenged them to propose any thing they could urge, to prove that a life of irreligion and debauchery was preferable to the fear, love, and worship of the eternal God, and a conduct agreeable to the precepts of his gospel. And he failed not to bear his testimony, from his own experience, (to one part of which many of them had been witnesses,) that after having run the widest round of sensual pleasure, with all the advantages the best constitution and spirits could give him, he had never tasted any thing that deserved to be called happiness, till he had made religion his refuge and his delight. He testified calmly and boldly the habitual serenity and peace which he now felt in his own breast, (for the most elevated delights he did not think fit to plead, lest they should be esteemed enthusiasm,) and the composure and pleasure with which he looked forward to objects which the gayest sinner must acknowledge to be equally unavoidable and dreadful.

I know not what might be attempted by some of the company in answer to this; but I well remember he told me that the master of the table, a person of a very frank and candid disposition, cut short the debate, and said, "Come, let us call another cause. We thought this man mad, and he is in good earnest proving that we are so." On the whole, this well-judged circumstance saved him a great deal of future trouble. When his former acquaintances observed that he was still conversible and innocently cheerful, and that he was immovable in his resolutions, they desisted from further importunity; and he has assured me, that instead of losing any one valuable friend by this change in his character, he found himself much more esteemed and regarded by many who could not persuade themselves to imitate his example.

I have not any memoirs of Colonel Gardiner's life, or of any other remarkable event befalling him in it, from the time of his return to England till his marriage in the year 1726, except the extracts which have been sent me from some letters, which he wrote to his religious friends during this interval, and which I cannot pass by without a more particular notice. It may be recollected, that in consequence of the reduction of that regiment of which he was major, he was out of commission from Nov. 10, 1718, till June 1, 1724; and, after he returned from Paris, I find all his letters during this period dated from London, where he continued in communion with the Christian society under the pastoral care of Dr. Calamy. As his good mother also belonged to the same, it is easy to imagine it must have been an unspeakable pleasure to her to have such frequent opportunities of conversing with such a son, of observing in his daily conduct and discourses the blessed effects of that change which divine grace had made in his heart, and of sitting down with him monthly at that sacred feast where Christians so frequently enjoy the divinest entertainments which they expect on this side heaven. I the rather mention this ordinance, because, as this excellent lady had a very high esteem for it, so she had an opportunity of attending it but the very Lord's day immediately preceding her death, which happened on Thursday, October 7, 1725, after her son had been removed from her almost a year. He had maintained her handsomely out of that very moderate income on which he subsisted since his regiment had been disbanded; and when she expressed her gratitude to him for it, he assured her (in one of the last letters she ever received from him) "that he esteemed it a great honour that God put it into his power to make what he called a very small acknowledgment of all her care for him, and especially of the many prayers she had offered on his account, which had already been remarkably answered, and the benefit of which he hoped ever to enjoy."

I apprehend that the Earl of Stair's regiment, to the majority of which he was promoted on the 20th of July, 1724, was then quartered in Scotland; for all the letters in my hand, from that time to the 6th of February, 1726, are dated from thence, and particularly from Douglas, Stranraer, Hamilton, and Ayr. But I have the pleasure to find, from comparing these with others of an earlier date from London and the neighbouring parts, that neither the detriment which he must suffer by being so long out of commission, nor the hurry of affairs while charged with it, could prevent or interrupt that intercourse with Heaven, which was his daily feast, and his daily strength.

These were most eminently the happy years of his life; for he had learned to estimate his happiness, not by the increase of honour, or the possession of wealth, or by what was much dearer to his generous heart than either, the converse of the dearest and worthiest human friends; but by nearness to God, and by opportunities of humble converse with him, in the lively exercise of contemplation, praise, and prayer. Now there was no period of his life in which he was more eminently favoured with these, nor do I find any of his letters so overflowing with transports of holy joy, as those which were dated during this time. There are indeed in some of them such very sublime passages, that I have been dubious whether I should communicate them to the public or not, lest I should administer matter of profane ridicule to some, who look upon all the elevations of devotion as contemptible enthusiasm. And it has also given me some apprehensions lest it should discourage some pious Christians, who, after having spent several years in the service of God, and in humble obedience to the precepts of his gospel, may not have attained to any such heights as these. But, on the whole, I cannot satisfy myself to suppress them; not only as I number some of them, considered in a devotional view, among the most extraordinary pieces of the kind I have ever met with; but as some of the most excellent and judicious persons I any where know, to whom I have read them, have assured me that they felt their hearts in an unusual manner impressed, quickened, and edified by them.

CHAPTER VI.

LETTERS.

I WILL therefore draw back the veil, and show my much honoured friend in his most secret recesses, that the world may see what those springs were, from whence issued that clear, permanent and living stream of wisdom, piety, and virtue, which so evidently ran through all that part of his life which was open to public observation. It is not to be imagined that letters written in the intimacy of Christian friendship, some of them with the most evident marks of haste, and amidst a variety of important public cares, should be adorned with any studied elegance of expression, about which the greatness of his soul would not allow him to be at any time very solicitous, for he generally (as far as I could observe) wrote as fast as his pen could move, which, happily both for him and his many friends, was very freely. Yet here the grandeur of his subject has sometimes clothed his ideas with a language more elevated than is ordinarily to be expected in an epistolary correspondence. The proud scorners who may deride sentiments and enjoyments like those which this truly great man so experimentally and pathetically describes, I pity from my heart, and grieve to think how unfit they must be for the hallelujahs of heaven, who pour contempt upon the nearest approaches to them; nor shall I think it any misfortune to share with so excellent a person their profane derision. It will be infinitely more than an equivalent for all that such ignorance and petulancy can think and say, if I may convince some, who are as yet strangers to religion, how real and how noble its delights are—if I may engage my pious readers to glorify God for so illustrious an instance of his grace—and finally, if I may quicken them, and, above all, may rouse my own too indolent spirit to follow with less unequal steps an example, to the sublimity of which, I fear, few of us shall, after all, be able fully to attain. And that we may not be too much discouraged under the deficiency, let it be recollected that few have the advantage of a temper naturally so warm; few have an equal command of retirement; and perhaps hardly any one who thinks himself most indebted to the riches and freedom of divine grace, can trace interpositions of it in all respects equally astonishing.

The first of these extraordinary letters which have fallen into my hand, is dated near three years after his conversion, and addressed to a lady of quality. I believe it is the first the major ever wrote, so immediately on the subject of his religious consolations and converse with God in devout retirement; for I well remember that he once told me he was so much afraid that something of spiritual pride should mingle itself with the relation of such kind of experiences, that he concealed them a long time; but observing with how much freedom the sacred writers open all the most secret recesses of their hearts, especially in the Psalms, his conscience began to be burdened, under an apprehension that, for the honour of God, and in order to engage the concurrent praises of some of his people, he ought to disclose them. On this he set himself to reflect who among all his numerous acquaintance seemed at once the most experienced Christians, (to whom, therefore, such things as he had to communicate might appear solid and credible,) and who the humblest. He quickly thought of the Lady Marchioness of Douglas in this view; and the reader may well imagine that it struck my mind very strongly, to think that now, more than twenty-four years after it was written, Providence should bring to my hands (as it has done within these few days) what I assuredly believe to be a genuine copy of that very letter, which I had not the least reason to expect I should ever have seen, when I learned from his own mouth, amidst the freedom of an accidental conversation, the occasion and circumstances of it. It is dated from London, July 21, 1722, and the very first lines of it relate to a remarkable circumstance which, from others of his letters, I find happened several times; I mean, that when he had received from any of his Christian friends a few lines which particularly affected his heart, he could not stay till the stated return of his devotional hour, but immediately retired to pray for them, and to give vent to those religious emotions of mind which such a correspondence raised. How invaluable was such a friend! and what great reason have those of us who once possessed a large share in his heart, and in those retired and sacred moments, to bless God for so singular a felicity; and to comfort ourselves in a pleasing hope that we may yet reap future blessings, as the harvest of those petitions which he can no more repeat.

His words are these:

"I was so happy as to receive yours just as I arrived, and had no sooner read it but I shut my door, and sought Him whom my soul loveth. I sought him, and found him; and would not let him go till he had blessed us all. It is impossible to find words to express what I obtained; but I suppose it was something like that which the disciples got, as they were going to Emmaus, when they said, 'Did not our hearts burn within us,' &c.; or rather like what Paul felt, when he could not tell whether he was in the body, or out of it."

He then mentions his dread of spiritual pride, from whence he earnestly prays that God may deliver and preserve him.

"This," says he, "would have hindered me from communicating these things, if I had not such an example before me as the man after God's own heart, saying, 'I will declare what God hath done for my soul;' and elsewhere, 'The humble shall hear thereof, and be glad.' Now I am well satisfied that your ladyship is of that number."

He then adds:

"I had no sooner finished this exercise," that is of prayer above mentioned, "but I sat down to admire the goodness of my God, that he would vouchsafe to influence by his free Spirit so undeserving a wretch as I, and to make me thus to mount up with eagles' wings. And here I was lost again, and got into an ocean, where I could find neither bound nor bottom; but was obliged to cry out with the apostle, 'O the breadth, the length, the depth, the height of the love of Christ, which passeth knowledge!' But if I give way to this strain I shall never have done. That the God of hope may fill you with all joy and peace in believing, that you may abound in hope through the power of the Holy Ghost, shall always be the prayer of him who is, with the greatest sincerity and respect, your Ladyship's," &c.

Another passage to the same purpose I find in a memorandum, which he seems to have written for his own use, dated Monday, March 11, which I perceive, from many concurrent circumstances, must have been in the year 1722—3.

"This day," says he, "having been to visit Mrs. G. at Hampstead, I came home about two, and read a sermon on these words, Psalm cxxx. 4, 'But there is forgiveness with thee, that thou mayest be feared;' about the latter end of which, there is a description of the miserable condition of those that are slighters of pardoning grace. From a sense of the great obligations I lie under to the Almighty God, who hath made me to differ from such, from what I was, and from the rest of my companions, I knelt down to praise his holy name; and I know not in my lifetime I ever lay lower in the dust, never having had a fuller view of my own unworthiness. I never pleaded more strongly the merits and intercession of Him who I know is worthy—never vowed more sincerely to be the Lord's, and to accept of Christ, as he is offered in the gospel, as my King, Priest, and Prophet—never had so strong a desire to depart, that I might sin no more; but 'my grace is sufficient,' curbed that desire. I never pleaded with greater fervency for the Comforter, which our blessed Lord hath promised shall abide with us for ever. For all which, I desire to ascribe glory &c. to Him that sitteth on the throne, and to the Lamb."

There are several others of his papers, speaking much the same language, which, had he kept a diary, would, I doubt not, have filled many sheets. I believe my devout readers would not soon be weary of reading extracts of this kind; but that I may not exceed in this part of my narrative, I shall mention only two more, each of them dated some years after; that is, one from Douglas,

April 1, 1725; and the other from Stranraer, 25th May following.

The former of these relates to the frame of his spirit on a journey; on the mention of which, I cannot but recollect how often I have heard him say that some of the most delightful days of his life were days in which he travelled alone, (that is, with only a servant at a distance,) when he could, especially in roads not much frequented, indulge himself in the pleasures of prayer and praise. In the exercise of this last, he was greatly assisted by several psalms and hymns which he had treasured up in his memory, and which he used not only to repeat aloud, but sometimes to sing. In reference to this, I remember the following passage, in a letter which he wrote to me many years after, when, on mentioning my ever dear and honoured friend the Rev. Dr. Watts, he says, "How often, in singing some of his psalms, hymns, or lyrics, on horseback and elsewhere, has the evil spirit been made to flee:

"'Whene'er my heart in tune was found,
'Like David's harp of solemn sound!'"

Such was the first of April above mentioned.

In the evening of that day he writes thus to an intimate friend :—

"What would I have given this day, upon the road, for paper, pen, and ink, when the Spirit of the Most High rested upon me! Oh for the pen of a ready writer, and the tongue of an angel, to declare what God hath done this day for my soul! But, in short, it is in vain to attempt it. All that I am able to say, is this, that my soul has been for some hours joining with the blessed spirits above in giving glory, and honour, and praise unto Him that sitteth upon the throne, and to the Lamb, for ever and ever. My praises began from a renewed view of Him whom I saw pierced for my transgressions. I summoned the whole hierarchy of heaven to join with me, and I am persuaded they all echoed back praise to the Most High. Yea, one would have thought the very larks joined me with emulation. Sure, then, I need not make use of many words to persuade you, that are his saints, to join me in blessing and praising his holy name." He concludes, "May the blessing of the God of Jacob rest upon you all! Adieu. Written in great haste, late and weary."

Scarcely can I here refrain from breaking out into more copious reflections on the exquisite pleasures of true religion, when risen to such eminent degrees, which can thus feast the soul in its solitude, and refresh it on journeys, and bring down so much of heaven to earth as this delightful letter expresses. But the remark is so obvious, that I will not enlarge upon it; but proceed to the other letter above mentioned, which was written the next month, on the Tuesday after a sacrament day.

He mentions the pleasure with which he had attended a preparation sermon the Saturday before; and then he adds:—

"I took a walk upon the mountains that are over against Ireland; and I persuade myself, that were I capable of giving you a description of what passed there, you would agree that I had much better reason to remember my God from the hills of Port Patrick than David from the land of Jordan, and of the Hermonites, from the hill of Mizar." I suppose he refers to the clearer discoveries of the gospel with which we are favoured. "In short," says he immediately afterwards, in that scripture phrase which had become so familiar to him, "I wrestled some hours with the Angel of the covenant, and made supplications to him with floods of tears, and cries—until I had almost expired; but he strengthened me so, that, like Jacob, I had power with God, and prevailed. This," adds he, "is but a very faint description; you will be more able to judge of it by what you have felt yourself upon the like occasions. After such preparatory work, I need not tell you how blessed the solemn ordinance of the Lord's supper proved to me; I hope it was so to many. You may believe I should have been exceeding glad, if my gracious Lord had ordered it so, that I might have made you a visit, as I proposed; but I am now glad it was ordered otherwise, since he hath caused so much of his goodness to pass before me. Were I to give you an account of the many favours my God hath loaded me with, since I parted from you, I must have taken up many days in nothing but writing. I hope you will join with me in praises for all the goodness he has shown to your unworthy brother in the Lord."

Such were the ardours and elevation of his soul. But while I record these memorials of them, I am very sensible that there are many who will be inclined to censure them as the flights of enthusiasm; for which reason, I must beg leave to add a remark or two on the occasion, which will be illustrated by several other extracts, which I shall introduce into the sequel of these memoirs. The one is, that he never pretends, in any of the passages cited above, or elsewhere, to have received from God any immediate revelations which should raise him above the ordinary methods of instruction, or discover any thing to him, whether of doctrines or facts. No man was further from pretending to predict future events, except from the moral prognostications of causes naturally tending to produce them, in tracing of which he had indeed an admirable sagacity, as I have seen in some very remarkable instances. Neither was he at all inclinable to govern himself by secret impulses upon his mind, leading him to things for which he could assign no reason but the impulse itself. Had he ventured, in a presumption on such secret agitations of mind, to teach or to do any thing not warranted by the dictates of sound sense and the word of God, I should readily have acknowledged him an enthusiast, unless he could have produced some other evidence than his own persuasion to have supported the authority of them. But these ardent expressions, which some may call enthusiasm, seem only to evince a heart deeply affected with a sense of the divine presence and perfections, and of that love which passeth knowledge, especially as manifested in our redemption by the Son of God, which did indeed inflame his whole soul. And he thought he might reasonably ascribe these strong impressions, to which men are generally such strangers, and of which he had long been entirely destitute, to the agency or influence of the Spirit of God upon his heart; and that, in proportion to the degree in which he felt them, he might properly say, God was present with him, and he conversed with God.* Now, when we consider the scriptural phrases of "walking with God," of "having communion with the Father and his Son Jesus Christ," of "Christ's coming to them that open the door of their hearts to him, and supping with them," of "God's shedding abroad his love in the heart by his Spirit," of "his coming with Jesus Christ, and making his abode with any man that loves him," of "his meeting him that worketh righteousness," of "his making us glad

* The ingenious and pious Mr. Grove (who, I think, was as little suspected of running into enthusiastical extremes as most divines I could name,) has a noble passage to this purpose in the sixth volume of his Posthumous Works, p. 40, 41, which, respect to the memory of both these excellent persons, inclines me to insert here. "How often are the good thoughts suggested," (viz. to the pure in heart,) "heavenly affections kindled and inflamed! How often is the Christian prompted to holy actions, drawn to his duty, restored, quickened, persuaded, in such a manner, that he would be unjust to the Spirit of God to question his agency in the whole! Yes, oh my soul! there is a Supreme Being, who governs the world, and is present with it, who takes up his more special habitation in good men, and is nigh to all who call upon him, to sanctify and assist them! Hast thou not felt him, oh my soul! like another soul, actuating thy faculties, exalting thy views, purifying thy passions, exciting thy graces, and begetting in thee an abhorrence of sin, and a love of holiness? Is not all this an argument of his presence, as truly as if thou didst see.

by the light of his countenance," and a variety of other equivalent expressions,—I believe we shall see reason to judge much more favourably of such expressions as those now in question, than persons who, themselves strangers to elevated devotion, perhaps converse but little with their Bible, are inclined to do; especially, if they have, as many such persons have, a temper that inclines them to cavil and find fault. And I must further observe, that amidst all those freedoms with which this eminent Christian opens his devout heart to the most intimate of his friends, he still speaks with profound awe and reverence of his Heavenly Father and his Saviour, and maintains (after the example of the sacred writers themselves,) a kind of dignity in his expressions, suitable to such a subject, without any of that fond familiarity of language, and degrading meanness of phrase, by which it is, especially of late, grown fashionable among some (who nevertheless I believe mean well,) to express their love and their humility.

On the whole, if habitual love to God, firm faith in the Lord Jesus Christ, a steady dependence on the divine promises, a full persuasion of the wisdom and goodness of all the dispensations of Providence, a high esteem for the blessings of the heavenly world, and a sincere contempt for the vanities of this, can properly be called enthusiasm, then was Colonel Gardiner indeed one of the greatest enthusiasts which our age has produced; and in proportion to the degree in which he was so, I must esteem him one of the wisest and happiest of mankind. Nor do I fear to tell the world that it is the design of my writing these memoirs, and of every thing else that I undertake in life, to spread this glorious and blessed enthusiasm, which I know to be the anticipation of heaven, as well as the most certain way to it.

But lest any should possibly imagine, that allowing the experiences which have been described above to have been ever so solid and important, yet there may be some appearances of boasting in so free a communication of them, I must add to what I have hinted in reference to this above, that I find in many of the papers before me very genuine expressions of the deepest humility and self-abasement, which indeed such holy converse with God in prayer and praise does, above all things in the world, tend to inspire and promote. Thus, in one of his letters he says, "I am but as a beast before him." In another he calls himself "a miserable hell-deserving sinner." And in another he cries out, "Oh, how good a master do I serve! but, alas, how ungrateful am I! What can be so astonishing as the love of Christ to us, unless it be the coldness of our sinful hearts towards such a Saviour?" There were many other clauses of the like nature, which I shall not set myself more particularly to trace through the variety of letters in which they occur.

It is a further instance of this unfeigned humility, that when (as his lady with her usual propriety of language expresses it in one of her letters to me concerning him,) "these divine joys and consolations were not his daily allowance," he, with equal freedom, in the confidence of Christian friendship, acknowledges and laments it. Thus, in the first letter I had the honour of receiving from him, dated from Leicester, July 9, 1739, after mentioning the blessing with which it had pleased God to attend my last address to him, and the influence it had upon his mind, he adds, "Much do I stand in need of every help to awaken me out of that spiritual deadness which seizes me so often. Once, indeed, it was quite otherwise with me, and that for many years:

"'Firm was my health, my day was bright,
And I presumed 'twould ne'er be night;
Fondly I said within my heart,
Pleasure and peace shall ne'er depart.
But I forgot, thine arm was strong,
Which made my mountain stand so long;
Soon as thy face began to hide,
My health was gone, my comforts died.'

And here," adds he, "lies my sin and my folly."

I mention this, that the whole matter may be seen just as it was, and that other Christians may not be discouraged if they feel some abatement of that fervour, and of those holy joys which they may have experienced during some of the first months or years of their spiritual life. But, with relation to the colonel, I have great reason to believe that those which he laments as his days of spiritual deadness were not unanimated; and that quickly after the date of this letter, and especially nearer the close of his life, he had further revivings, as the joyful anticipation in reserve of those better things which were then nearly approaching. And thus Mr. Spears, in the letter I mentioned above, tells us he related the matter to him, (for he studies as much as possible to retain the colonel's own words): "However," says he, "after that happy period of sensible communion, though my joys and enlargements were not so overflowing and sensible, yet I have had habitual real communion with God from that day to this"—the latter end of the year 1743—"and I know myself, and all that know me see, that through the grace of God, to which I ascribe all, my conversation has been becoming the gospel; and let me die whenever it shall please God, or wherever it shall be, I am sure I shall go to the mansions of eternal glory," &c. This is perfectly agreeable to the manner in which he used to speak to me on this head, which we have talked over frequently and largely.

In this connection I hope my reader will forgive my inserting a little story which I received from a very worthy minister in Scotland, and which I shall give in his own words: "In this period," meaning that which followed the first seven years after his conversion, "when his complaint of comparative deadness and languor in religion began, he had a dream, which, though he had no turn at all for taking notice of dreams, yet made a very strong impression upon his mind. He imagined he saw his blessed Redeemer on earth, and that he was following him through a large field, following him whom his soul loved, but much troubled, because he thought his blessed Lord did not speak to him, till he came up to the gate of a burying-place, when, turning about, he smiled upon him in such a manner as filled his soul with the most ravishing joy, and on after reflection animated his faith in believing that whatever storms and darkness he might meet with in the way, at the hour of death his glorious Redeemer would lift up upon him the light of his life-giving countenance." My correspondent adds a circumstance for which he makes some apology, as what may seem whimsical, and yet made some impression on the colonel,—"that there was a remarkable resemblance in the field in which this brave man met his death, and that he had represented to him in the dream." I did not fully understand this at first; but a passage in that letter from Mr. Spears, which I have mentioned more than once, has cleared it:

"Now observe, sir, this seems to be a literal description of the place where this Christian hero ended his sorrows and conflicts, and from which he entered triumphantly into the joy of his Lord; for, after he fell in the battle, fighting gloriously for his king and the cause of his God, his wounded body, while life was yet remaining, was carried from the field of battle by the east side of his own enclosure, till he came to the church-yard of Tranent, and was brought to the minister's house, where, about an hour after, he breathed out his soul into the hands of his Lord, and was conducted to his presence, where there is fulness of joy, without any cloud or interruption, for ever."

I well know that in dreams there are diverse vanities, and readily acknowledge that nothing certain could be inferred from this; yet it seems at least to show which way the imagination was working even in sleep; and I cannot think it unworthy of a wise and good man sometimes to reflect with complacency on any images which, passing through his mind even in that state, may tend either to express or to quicken his love to the great Saviour. Those eminently pious divines of the Church of England, Bishop Bull and Bishop Kenn, do both intimate it as their opinion that it may be a part of the service of ministering angels to suggest devout dreams.*

* Bishop Bull has these remarkable words: "Although I am no doater on dreams, yet I verily believe that some dreams are monitory, above the power of fancy, and impressed upon us by some superior influence. For of such dreams we have plain and undeniable instances in history, both sacred and profane, and in our own age and observation. Nor shall I so value the laughter of sceptics, and the scoffs of epicureans, as to be ashamed to profess that I myself have had some convincing experiments of such impressions."—*Bishop Bull's Sermons and Discourses*, Vol. II, pp. 489, 490.

and I know that the worthy person of whom I speak was well acquainted with that evening hymn of the latter of those excellent writers which has these lines:

> "Lord, lest the tempter me surprise,
> Watch over thine own sacrifice!
> All loose, all idle thoughts cast out;
> And make my very *dreams* devout!"

Nor would it be difficult to produce other passages much to the same purpose,* if it would not be deemed too great a digression from our subject, and too laboured a vindication of a little incident of very small importance when compared with most of those which make up this narrative.†

* If I mistake not, the same Bishop Kenn is the author of a *midnight hymn* concluding with these words:

> "May my ethereal Guardian kindly spread
> His wings, and from the tempter screen my head;
> Grant of celestial light some piercing beams,
> To bless my sleep, and sanctify my dreams!"

As he certainly was of those exactly parallel lines:

> Oh may my Guardian, while I sleep,
> Close to my bed his vigils keep;
> His love angelical distil,
> Stop all the avenues of ill!
> May he celestial joys rehearse,
> And thought to thought with me converse!"

† See Appendix.

CHAPTER VII.

DOMESTIC RELATIONS.

I MEET not with any other remarkable event relating to Major Gardiner, which can properly be introduced here, till 1726, when, on the 11th of July, he was married to the Right Hon. Lady Frances Erskine, daughter to the late Earl of Buchan, by whom he had thirteen children, five only of which survived their father, two sons and three daughters, whom I cannot mention without the most fervent prayers to God for them, that they may always behave worthy the honour of being descended from such parents, and that the God of their father and of their mother may make them perpetually the care of his providence, and yet more eminently happy in the constant and abundant influences of his grace.

As her ladyship is still living,* (and for the sake of her dear offspring, and numerous friends, may she long be spared,) I shall not here indulge myself in saying any thing of her, except it be that the colonel assured me, when he had been happy in this intimate relation to her more than fourteen years, that the greatest imperfection he knew in her character was, "that she valued and loved him much more than he deserved." Little did he think, in the simplicity of heart with which he spoke this, how high an encomium he was making upon her, and how lasting an honour such a testimony must leave upon her name, long as the memory of it shall continue.

As I do not intend in these memoirs a laboured essay on the character of Colonel Gardiner, digested under the various virtues and graces which Christianity requires, (which would, I think, be a little too formal for a work of this kind, and would give it such an air of panegyric as would neither suit my design, nor be at all likely to render it more useful,) I shall now mention what I have either observed in him, or heard concerning him, with regard to

* In the year 1746.

those domestic relations which commenced about this time, or very soon after. And here my reader will easily conclude that the resolution of Joshua was from the first adopted and declared, "As for me and my house, we will serve the Lord." It will naturally be supposed, that as soon as he had a house, he erected an altar in it; that the word of God was read there, and prayers and praises were constantly offered. These were not to be omitted on account of any guest; for he esteemed it a part of due respect to those that remained under his roof to take it for granted they would look upon it as a very bad compliment to imagine they would have been obliged by neglecting the duties of religion on their account. As his family increased, he had a minister statedly resident in his house, who discharged both the office of a tutor to his children, and of a chaplain, and who was always treated with a becoming kindness and respect. But, in his absence, the colonel himself led the devotions of the family; and they were happy who had an opportunity of knowing with how much solemnity, fervour, and propriety he did it. He was constant in attendance upon public worship, in which an exemplary care was taken that the children and servants might accompany the heads of the family. And how he would have resented the non-attendance of any member of it may easily be conjectured from a free but lively passage in a letter to one of his intimate friends, on an occasion which it is not material to mention. "Oh, sir, had a child of yours under my roof but once neglected the public worship of God when he was able to attend it, I should have been ready to conclude he had been distracted, and should have thought of shaving his head, and confining him in a dark room."

He always treated his lady with a manly tenderness, giving her the most natural evidences of a cordial, habitual esteem, and expressing a most affectionate sympathy with her under the infirmities of a very delicate constitution, much broken, at least towards the latter years of their marriage. He had at all times a most faithful care of all her interests, and especially those relating to the state of religion in her mind. His conversation and his letters concurred to cherish those sublime ideas which Christianity suggests, to promote our submission to the will of God, to teach us to centre our happiness in the great Author of our being, and to live by faith in the invisible world. These, no doubt, were frequently the subjects of mutual discourse; and many letters, which her ladyship has had the goodness to communicate to me, are most convincing evidences of the degree in which this noble and most friendly care filled his mind in the days of their separation—days which so entire a mutual affection must have rendered exceedingly painful, had they not been supported by such exalted sentiments of piety, and sweetened by daily communion with an ever-present and ever-gracious God.

The necessity of being so many months together distant from his family hindered him from many of those condescending labours in cultivating the minds of his children in early life, which, to a soul so benevolent, so wise, and so zealous, would undoubtedly have afforded a very exquisite pleasure. The care of his worthy consort, who well knew that it is one of the brightest parts of a mother's character, and one of the most important views in which the sex can be considered, made him the easier under such a circumstance; but when he was with them, he failed not to instruct and admonish them; and the constant deep sense with which he spoke of divine things, and the real unaffected indifference which he always showed for what this vain world is most ready to admire, were excellent lessons of daily wisdom, which I hope they will recollect with advantage in every future scene of life. And I have seen such hints in his letters relating to them, as plainly show with how great a weight they lay on his mind, and how highly he desired, above all things, that they might be the faithful disciples of Christ, and acquainted betimes with the unequalled pleasures and blessings of religion. He thought an excess of delicacy and of indulgence one of the most dangerous faults in education, by which he every where saw great numbers of young people undone; yet he was solicitous to guard against a severity which might terrify or discourage; and though he endeavoured to take all prudent precautions to prevent the commission of faults, yet, when they had been committed, and there seemed to be a sense of them, he was always ready to make the most candid allowances for the thoughtlessness of unripened years, and tenderly to cherish every purpose of a more proper conduct for the time to come.

It was to perceive that the openings of genius in the young branches of his family gave him great delight, and that he had a secret ambition to see them excel in what they undertook. Yet he was greatly cautious over his heart, lest it should be too fondly attached to them; and as he was one of the most eminent proficients I ever knew in the blessed science of resignation to the divine will, so there was no effect of that resignation which appeared to me more admirable than what related to the life of his children. An experience, which no length of time will ever efface out of my memory, has so sensibly taught me how difficult it is fully to support the Christian character here, that I hope my reader will pardon me (I am sure, at least, the heart of wounded parents will,) if I dwell a little longer upon so interesting a subject.*

When he was in Herefordshire in July, 1734, it pleased God to visit his little family with the small-pox. Five days before the date of the letter I am just going to mention, he had received the agreeable news that there was a prospect of the recovery of his son, then under that awful visitation; and he had been expressing

* See Appendix.

his thankfulness for it in a letter which he had sent away but a few hours before he was informed of his death, the surprise of which, in this connection, must naturally be very great. But behold (says the reverend and worthy person from whom I received the copy) his truly filial submission to the will of his Heavenly Father, in the following lines addressed to the dear partner of his affliction: "Your resignation to the will of God under this dispensation gives me more joy than the death of the child has given me sorrow. He, to be sure, is happy; and we shall go to him, though he shall not return to us. Oh that we had our latter end always in view! We shall soon follow; and oh, what reason have we to long for that glorious day when we shall get quit of this body of sin and death under which we now groan, and which renders this life so wretched! I desire to bless God that —— (another of his children) is in so good a way; but I have resigned her. We must not choose for ourselves; and it is well we must not, for we should often make a very bad choice, and therefore it is our wisdom, as well as our duty, to leave all with a gracious God, who hath promised that all things shall work together for good to them that love him; and he is faithful that hath promised, who will infallibly perform it, if our unbelief does not stand in the way."

The greatest trial of this kind that he ever bore, was in the removal of his second son, who was one of the most amiable and promising children that has been known. The dear little creature was the darling of all that knew him; and promised very fair, so far as a child could be known by its doings, to have been a great ornament to the family, and blessing to the public. The suddenness of the stroke must, no doubt, render it the more painful; for this beloved child was snatched away by an illness which seized him but about fifteen hours before it carried him off. He died in the month of October 1733, at near six years old. Their friends were ready to fear that his affectionate parents would be almost overwhelmed at such a loss; but the happy father had so firm a persuasion that God had received the dear little one to the felicities of the celestial world, and at the same time had so strong a sense of the divine goodness in taking one of his children, and that, too, one who lay so near his heart, so early to himself, that the sorrows of nature were quite swallowed up in the sublime joy which these considerations administered. When he reflected what human life is—how many its snares and temptations are—and how frequently children who once promised very well are insensibly corrupted, and at length undone, with Solomon he blessed the dead already dead, more than the living who were yet alive, and felt unspeakable pleasure in looking after the lovely infant, as safely and delightfully lodged in the house of its Heavenly Father. Yea, he assured me that his heart was at this time so entirely taken up with these views, that he was afraid they who did not thoroughly know him might suspect that he was deficient in the natural affections of a parent, while thus borne above the anguish of them by the views which faith administered to him, and which divine grace supported in his soul.

So much did he, on one of the most trying occasions of life, manifest of the temper of a glorified saint, and to such happy purposes did he retain those lessons of submission to God, and acquiescence in him, which I remember he once inculcated in a letter he wrote to a lady of quality under the apprehension of a breach in her family with which Providence seemed to threaten her, which I am willing to insert here, though a little out of what might seem its most proper place rather than entirely to omit it. It is dated from London, June 16, 1722, when, speaking of the dangerous illness of a dear relative, he has these words: "When my mind runs hither," that is, to God, as its refuge and strong defence, (as the connection plainly determines it,) "I think I can bear any thing, the loss of all, the loss of health, of relations, on whom I depend, and whom I love, all that is dear to me, without repining or murmuring. When I think that God orders, disposes, and manages all things according to the counsel of his own will; when I think of the extent of his providence, that it reaches to the minutest things; then, though a useful friend or dear relative be snatched away by death, I recall myself, and check my thoughts with these considerations: Is he not God from everlasting, and to everlasting? And has he not promised to be a God to me?—a God in all his attributes, a God in all his persons, a God in all his creatures and providences? And shall I dare to say, What shall I do? Was not he the infinite cause of all I met with in the creatures? And were not they the finite effects of his infinite love and kindness? I have daily experienced that the instrument was, and is, what God makes it to be; and I know that this 'God hath the hearts of all men in his hands, and the earth is the Lord's, and the fulness thereof.' If this earth be good for me, I shall have it; for my Father hath it all in possession. If favour in the eyes of men be good for me, I shall have it; for the spring of every motion in the heart of man is in God's hand. My dear —— seems now to be dying; but God is all-wise, and every thing is done by him for the best. Shall I hold back any thing that is his own, when he requires it? No, God forbid! When I consider the excellency of his glorious attributes, I am satisfied with all his dealings." I perceive by the introduction, and by what follows, that most, if not all of this, is a quotation from something written by a lady; but whether from some manuscript or printed book, whether exactly transcribed or quoted from memory, I cannot determine; and therefore I thought proper to insert it, as the major (for that was the office he bore then,) by thus interweaving it with his letter, makes it his own, and as it seems to express in a very lively manner the principles which bore him on to a conduct so truly great and heroic, in circumstances that have overwhelmed many a heart that could have faced danger and death with the greatest intrepidity.

I return now to consider his character in the domestic relation of a master, on which I shall not enlarge. It is, however, proper to remark, that as his habitual meekness and command of his passions prevented indecent sallies of ungoverned anger towards those in the lowest state of subjection to him, by which some in high life do strangely debase themselves, and lose much of their authority, so the natural greatness of his mind made him solicitous to render their inferior stations as easy as he could; and so much the rather, because he considered all the children of Adam as standing upon a level before their great Creator, and had also a deeper sense of the dignity and worth of every immortal soul, how meanly soever it might chance to be lodged, than most persons I have known. This engaged him to give his servants frequent religious exhortations and instructions, as I have been assured by several who were so happy as to live with him under that character. One of his first letters, after he entered on his Christian course, expresses the same disposition; in which, with great tenderness, he recommends a servant, who was in a bad state of health, to his mother's care, as he was well acquainted with her condescending temper; mentioning at the same time, the endeavours he had used to promote his preparations for a better world, under an apprehension that he would not continue long in this. We shall have an affecting instance of the prevalence of the same disposition in the closing scene of his life, and indeed in the last words he ever spoke, which expressed his generous solicitude for the safety of a faithful servant who was then near him.

CHAPTER VIII.

CONDUCT AS AN OFFICER.

As it was a few years after his marriage that he was promoted to the rank of lieutenant-colonel, in which he continued till he had a regiment of his own, I shall, for the future, speak of him by that title; and I may not, perhaps, find any more proper place in which to mention what it is proper for me to say of his behaviour and conduct as an officer. I shall not here enlarge on his bravery in the field, though, as I have heard from others, that was very remarkable—I say from others, for I never heard any thing of the kind from himself, nor knew, till after his death, that he was present at almost every battle that was fought in Flanders while the illustrious Duke of Marlborough commanded the allied army there. I have also been assured from several very credible persons, some of whom were eye-witnesses, that at the skirmish with the rebels at Preston in Lancashire, (thirty years before that engagement at the other Preston which deprived us of this gallant guardian of his country,) he signalized himself very particularly; for he headed a small body of men, I think about twelve, and set fire to the barricado of the rebels, in the face of their whole army, while they were pouring in their shot, by which eight of the twelve that attended him fell. This was the last action of the kind in which he was engaged before the long peace which ensued; and who can express how happy it was for him, and indeed for his country, of which he was ever so mindful, and in his latter years so important a friend, that he did not then fall, when the profaneness which mingled itself with this martial rage seemed to rend the heavens, and shocked some other military gentlemen who were not very remarkable for their caution in this respect.

But I insist not on things of this nature, which the true greatness of his soul would hardly ever permit him to mention, unless when it tended to illustrate the divine care over him in these extremities of danger, and the grace of God in calling him from so abandoned a state. It is well known that the character of

10*

an officer is not to be approved in the day of combat only. Colonel Gardiner was truly sensible that every day brought its duties along with it, and he was constantly careful that no pretence of amusement, friendship, or even devotion itself, might prevent their being properly discharged.

I doubt not that the noble persons in whose regiments he was lieutenant-colonel, will always be ready to bear an honourable and grateful testimony to his exemplary diligence and fidelity in all that related to the care of the troops over which he was set, whether in regard to the men or the horses. He knew that it is incumbent on those who have the honour of presiding over others, whether in civil, ecclesiastical, or military offices, not to content themselves with doing only so much as may preserve them from the reproach of gross and visible neglect; but seriously to consider how much they can possibly do without going out of their proper sphere, to serve the public, by the due inspection of those committed to their care. The duties of the closet and of the sanctuary were so adjusted as not to interfere with those of the parade, or any other place where the welfare of the regiment called him. On the other hand, he was solicitous not to suffer these things to interfere with religion, a due attendance on which he apprehended to be the surest method of attaining all desirable success in every other interest and concern in life. He therefore abhorred every thing that looked like a contrivance to keep his soldiers employed with their horses and their arms at the seasons of public worship—an indecency which I wish there were no room to mention. Far from that, he used to have them drawn up just before it began, and from the parade they went off to the house of God. He understood the rights of conscience too well to impose his own particular profession in religion on others, or to treat those who differed from him in the choice of its modes, the less kindly or respectfully on that account. But as most of his own company, and many of the rest, chose (when in England) to attend him to the dissenting chapel, he used to march them up thither in due time, so as to be there before the worship began. And I must do them the justice to say, that so far as I could ever discern, when I have seen them in large numbers before me, they behaved with as much reverence, gravity, and decorum, during the time of divine service, as any of the worshippers.

That his remarkable care to maintain good discipline among them (of which we shall afterwards speak) might be the more effectual, he made himself on all proper occasions accessible to them, and expressed a great concern for their interests, which, being genuine and sincere, naturally discovered itself in a variety of instances. I remember I had once occasion to visit one of his dragoons in his last illness at Harborough, and I found the man upon the borders of eternity—a circumstance which, as he apprehended himself, must add some peculiar weight and credibility to his discourse. He then told me, in his colonel's absence, that he questioned not that he should have everlasting reason to bless God on Colonel Gardiner's account, for he had been a father to him in all his interests, both temporal and spiritual. He added, that he had visited him, almost every day during his illness, with religious advice and instruction, and had also taken care that he should want for nothing that might conduct to the recovery of his health. He did not speak of this as the result of any particular attachment to him, but as the manner in which he was accustomed to treat those under his command. It is no wonder that this engaged their affection to a very great degree; and I doubt not that if he had fought the fatal battle of Prestonpans at the head of that gallant regiment of which he had the care for so many years, and which is allowed by most unexceptionable judges to be one of the finest in the British service, and consequently in the world, he had been supported in a much different manner, and had found a much greater number who would have rejoiced in an opportunity of making their own breasts a barrier in the defence of his.

It could not but greatly endear him to his soldiers, that so far as preferments lay in his power, or were under his influence, they were distributed according to merit. This he knew to be as much the dictate of prudence as equity. I find from one of his letters before me, dated but a few months after his conversion, that he was solicited to use his interest with the Earl of Stair in favour of one whom he judged a very worthy person; and that it had been suggested by another, who recommended him, that if he succeeded, he might expect some handsome acknowledgment. But he answers with some degree of indignation, "Do you imagine I am to be bribed to do justice?" For such it seems he esteemed it, to confer the favour which was asked from him on one so deserving. Nothing can more effectually tend to humble the enemies of a state, than that such maxims should universally prevail in it; and if they do not prevail, the worthiest men in an army or a fleet may sink under repeated discouragements, and the basest exalted, to the infamy of the public, and perhaps to its ruin.

In the midst of all the gentleness which Colonel Gardiner exercised towards his soldiers, he made it very apparent that he knew how to reconcile the tenderness of a really faithful and condescending friend with the authority of a commander. Perhaps hardly any thing conduced more generally to the maintaining of this authority, than the strict decorum and good manners with which he treated even the private gentlemen of his regiment; which has always a great efficacy in keeping inferiors at a proper distance, and forbids, in the least offensive manner, familiarities which degrade the superior, and enervate his influence. The calmness and steadiness of his behaviour on all occasions also greatly tended to the same purpose. He knew how mean a man looks in the transports of passion, and would not use so much freedom with many of his men as to fall into such transports before them, well knowing that persons in the lowest rank of life are aware how unfit *they* are to govern others, who cannot govern themselves. He was also sensible how necessary it is in all who preside over others, and especially in military officers, to check irregularities when they first begin to appear; and, that he might be able to do so, he kept a strict inspection over his soldiers; in which it was observed, that as he generally chose to reside among them as much as he could, (though in circumstances which sometimes occasioned him to deny himself in some interests which were very dear to him,) so, when they were around him, he seldom staid long in a place; but was frequently walking the streets, and looking into their quarters and stables, as well as reviewing and exercising them himself. It has often been observed that the regiment to which he was so many years lieutenant-colonel, was one of the most regular and orderly regiments in the public service, so that perhaps none of our dragoons were more welcome to the towns where their character was known. Yet no such bodies of men are so blameless in their conduct but something will be found, especially among such considerable numbers, worthy of censure, and sometimes of punishment. This Colonel Gardiner knew how to inflict with a becoming resolution, and with all the severity which he judged necessary—a severity the more awful and impressive, as it was always attended with meekness; for he well knew that when things are done in a passion, it seems only an accidental circumstance that they are acts of justice, and that such indecencies greatly obstruct the ends of punishment, both as to reforming offenders, and to deterring others from an imitation of their faults.

One instance of his conduct, which happened at Leicester, and which was related by the person chiefly concerned to a worthy friend from whom I had it, I cannot forbear inserting. While part of the regiment was encamped in the neighbourhood of that place, the colonel went incognito to the camp in the middle of the night; for he sometimes lodged at his quarters in the town. One of the sentinels then on duty had abandoned his post, and, on being seized, broke out into some oaths and profane execrations against those that discovered him—a crime of which the colonel had the greatest abhorrence, and on which he never failed to animadvert. The man afterwards appeared much ashamed and concerned for what he had done. But the colonel ordered him to be brought early the next morning to his own quarters, where he had prepared a picket, on which he appointed him a private sort of penance; and while he was put upon it, he discoursed with him seriously and tenderly upon the evils and aggravations of his fault, admonished him of the divine displeasure which he had incurred, and urged him to argue, from the pain which he then felt, how infinitely more dreadful it must be to "fall into the hands of the living God," and, indeed, to meet the terrors of that damnation which he had been accustomed impiously to call for on himself and his companions. The result of this proceeding was, that the offender accepted his punishment, not only with submission, but with thankfulness. He went away with a more cordial affection for his colonel than he ever had before, and spoke of the circumstance some years after to my friend, in such a manner that there seemed reason to hope it had been instrumental in producing a change not only in his life, but in his heart.

There cannot, I think, be a more proper place

for mentioning the great reverence this excellent officer always expressed for the name of the blessed God, and the zeal with which he endeavoured to suppress, and if possible to extirpate, that detestable sin of swearing and cursing which is every where so common, and especially among our military men. He often declared, at the head of his regiment, his sentiments with respect to this enormity, and urged his captains and their subalterns to take the greatest care that they did not give the sanction of their example to that which by their office they were obliged to punish in others. Indeed his zeal on these occasions wrought in a very active, and sometimes in a remarkably successful manner, not only among his equals, but sometimes among his superiors too. An instance of this in Flanders I shall have an opportunity hereafter to produce; at present I shall only mention his conduct in Scotland a little before his death, as I have it from a very valuable young minister of that country, on whose testimony I can thoroughly depend; and I wish it may excite many to imitation.

The commanding officer of the king's forces then about Edinburgh, with the other colonels, and several other gentlemen of rank in their respective regiments, favoured him with their company at Bankton, and took dinner with him. He too well foresaw what might happen amid such a variety of tempers and characters; and fearing lest his conscience might have been ensnared by a sinful silence, or that, on the other hand, he might seem to pass the bounds of decency, and infringe upon the laws of hospitality by animadverting on guests so justly entitled to his regard, he happily determined on the following method of avoiding each of these difficulties. As soon as they were come together, he addressed them with a great deal of respect, and at the same time with a very frank and determined air, telling them that he had the honour in that district to be a justice of the peace, and consequently that he was sworn to put the law in execution, and, among the rest, those against swearing; that he could not execute them upon others with any confidence, or by any means approve himself a man of impartiality and integrity to his own heart, if he suffered them to be broken in his presence by persons of any rank whatsoever; and that therefore he entreated all the gentlemen who then honoured him with their company that they would please to be upon their guard, and that if any oath or curse should escape them, he hoped they would consider his legal animadversion upon it as a regard to the duties of his office and the dictates of his conscience, and not as owing to any want of deference to them.

The commanding officer immediately supported him in this declaration, as entirely becoming the station in which he was, assuring him that he would be ready to pay the penalty, if he inadvertently transgressed; and when Colonel Gardiner on any occasion stepped out of the room, he himself undertook to be the guardian of the law in his absence; and as one of the inferior officers offended during this time, he informed the colonel, so that the fine was exacted and given to the poor,* with the universal approbation of the company. The story spread in the neighbourhood, and was perhaps applauded

* It is observable that the money which was forfeited on this account by his own officers, whom he never spared, or by any others of his soldiers who rather chose to pay than submit to corporal punishment, was, by the colonel's order, laid by in a bank till some of the private men fell sick, and then it was laid out in providing them with proper help and accommodations in their distress.

highly by many who wanted the courage to "go and do likewise." But it may be said, with the utmost propriety, of the worthy person of whom I write, that he feared the face of no man living where the honour of God was concerned. In all such cases he might be justly said, in Scripture phrase, "to set his face like a flint;" and I assuredly believe, that had he been in the presence of a sovereign prince who had been guilty of this fault, his looks at least would have testified his grief and surprise, if he had apprehended it unfit to have borne his testimony in any other way.

Lord Cadogan's regiment of dragoons, during the time he was lieutenant-colonel of it, was quartered in a variety of places, both in England and Scotland, from many of which I have letters before me; particularly from Hamilton, Ayr, Carlisle, Hereford, Maidenhead, Leicester, Warwick, Coventry, Stamford, Harborough, Northampton, and several other places, especially in our inland parts. The natural consequence was, that the colonel, whose character was on many accounts so very remarkable, had a very extensive acquaintance; and I believe I may certainly say, that wherever he was known by persons of wisdom and worth, he was proportionably respected, and left behind him traces of unaffected devotion, humility, benevolence, and zeal for the support and advancement of religion and virtue.

The equable tenor of his mind in these respects is illustrated by his letters from several of these places; and though I have but comparatively a small number of them now in my hands, yet they will afford some valuable extracts; which I shall therefore here lay before my reader, that he may the better judge as to the colonel's real character in particulars which I have already mentioned, or which may hereafter occur.

In a letter to his lady, dated from Carlisle, November 19, 1733, when he was on his journey to Herefordshire, he breathes out his grateful, cheerful soul in these words:

"I bless God I was never better in my lifetime, and I wish I could be so happy as to hear the same of you: or rather, in other words, to hear that you have obtained an entire trust in God. That would infallibly keep you in perfect peace, for the God of truth has promised it. Oh, how ought we to be longing 'to be with Christ,' which is infinitely better than any thing we can propose here! to be there, where no mountains shall separate between God and our souls. And I hope it will be some addition to our happiness, that you and I shall be separated no more; but that as we have joined in singing the praises of our glorious Redeemer here, we shall sing them in a much higher key through an endless eternity. Oh eternity, eternity! What a wonderful thought is eternity!"

From Leicester, August 6, 1739, he writes thus to his lady:

"Yesterday I was at the Lord's table, where you and the children were not forgotten. But how wonderfully was I assisted when I came home, to plead for you all with many tears." And then, speaking of some intimate friends who were impatient (as I suppose by the connection) for his return to them, he takes occasion to observe the necessity of endeavouring to compose our minds, and say with the Psalmist, "My soul, wait thou only upon God." Afterwards, speaking of one of his children, who he heard had made a commendable progress in learning, he expresses his satisfaction, and adds:—"But how much greater joy would it give me to hear that he was greatly advanced in the school of Christ! Oh that our children may but be wise unto salvation, and may grow in grace as they do in stature!"

These letters, which to so familiar a friend evidently lay open the heart, and show the ideas and affections which were lodged deepest there, are sometimes taken up with an account of sermons he had attended, and the impression they had made upon his mind. I shall mention only one, as a specimen of many more, which was dated from a place called Cohorn, April 15:

"We had here a minister from Wales, who gave us two excellent discourses on the love of Christ to us, as an argument to engage our love to him. And indeed, next to the greatness of his love to us, methinks there is nothing so astonishing as the coldness of our love to him. Oh that he would shed abroad his love upon our hearts by his Holy Spirit, that ours might be kindled into a flame! May God enable you to trust in Him, and then you will be kept in perfect peace!"

We have met with many traces of that habitual gratitude to the blessed God, as his Heavenly Father and constant friend, which made his life probably one of the happiest that ever was spent on earth. I cannot omit one more, which appears to me the more worthy of notice, as being a short turn in as hasty a letter as any I remember to have seen of his, which he wrote from Leicester in June, 1739. "I am now under the deepest sense of the many favours the Almighty has bestowed upon me. Surely you will help me to celebrate the praises of our gracious God and kind benefactor." This exuberance of grateful affection, which, while it was almost every hour pouring itself forth before God in the most genuine and emphatical language, felt itself still as it were straitened for want of a sufficient vent, and therefore called on others to help him with their concurrent praises, appears to me the most glorious and happy state in which a human soul can find itself on this side heaven.

Such was the temper which this excellent man appears to have carried along with him through such a variety of places and circumstances; and the whole of his deportment was suitable to these impressions. Strangers were agreeably struck with his first appearance, there being much of the Christian, the well-bred man, and the universal friend in it; and as they came more intimately to know him, they discovered more and more the uniformity and consistency of his whole temper and behaviour; so that whether he made only a visit for a few days to any place, or continued there for many weeks or months, he was always beloved and esteemed, and spoken of with that honourable testimony, from persons of the most different denominations and parties, which nothing but true sterling worth, (if I may be allowed the expression,) and that in an eminent degree, can secure.

CHAPTER IX.

INTIMACY WITH THE AUTHOR.

Of the justice of this testimony, which I had so often heard from a variety of persons, I myself began to be a witness about the time when the last mentioned letter was dated. In this view, I believe I shall never forget that happy day, June 13, 1739, when I first met him at Leicester. I remember I happened that day to preach a lecture from Psalm cxix. 158, "I beheld the transgressors, and was grieved because they kept not thy law." I was large in describing that mixture of indignation and grief (strongly expressed by the original words there) with which a good man looks on the daring transgressors of the divine law; and in tracing the causes of that grief, as arising from a regard to the divine honour, and the interest of a Redeemer, and a compassionate concern for the misery which such offenders bring on themselves, and for the mischief they do to the world about them, I little thought how exactly I was drawing Colonel Gardiner's character under each of those heads; and I have often reflected upon it as a happy providence which opened a much speedier way than I could have expected to the breast of one of the most amiable and useful friends whom I ever expect to find upon earth. We afterwards sang a hymn which brought over again some of the leading thoughts in the sermon, and struck him so strongly, that on obtaining a copy of it, he committed it to memory, and used to repeat it with so forcible an accent as showed how much every line expressed his very soul. In this view, the reader will pardon my inserting it, especially as I know not when I may get time to publish a volume of these serious though artless compositions, which I sent him in manuscript some years ago, and to which I have since made very large additions:

Arise, my tenderest thoughts arise,
To torrents melt my streaming eyes!
And thou, my heart, with anguish feel
Those evils which thou canst not heal!

See human nature sunk in shame!
See scandal poured on Jesus' name!
The Father wounded through the Son!
The world abused—the soul undone!

See the short course of vain delight
Closing in everlasting night!
In flames that no abatement know,
The briny tears for ever flow.

My God, I feel the mournful scene;
My bowels yearn o'er dying men:
And fain my pity would reclaim,
And snatch the firebrands from the flame.

But feeble my compassion proves,
And can but weep where most it loves;
Thine own all-saving arm employ,
And turn these drops of grief to joy!

The colonel, immediately after the conclusion of the service, met me in the vestry, and embraced me in the most obliging and affectionate manner, as if there had been a long friendship between us,—assured me that he had for some years been intimately acquainted with my writings, and desired that we might concert measures for spending some hours together before I left the town. I was so happy as to be able to secure an opportunity of doing it; and I must leave it upon record, that I cannot recollect I was ever equally edified by any conversation I remember to have enjoyed. We passed that evening and the next morning together, and it is impossible for me to describe the impression which the interview left upon my heart. I rode alone all the remainder of the day; and it was my unspeakable happiness that I was alone, since I could no longer be with him; for I can hardly conceive what other company would not then have been an encumbrance. The views which he gave me even then, (for he began to repose a most obliging confidence in me, though he concealed some of the most extraordinary circumstances of the methods by which he had been recovered to God and happiness,) with those cordial sentiments of evangelical piety and extensive goodness which he poured out into my bosom with so endearing a freedom, fired my very soul; and I hope I may truly say (which I wish and pray that many of my readers may also adopt for themselves) that I glorified God in him. Our epistolary correspondence immediately commenced upon my return; and though, through the multiplicity of business on both sides, it suffered many interruptions, it was in some degree the blessing of all the following years of my life, till he fell by those unreasonable and wicked men who had it in their hearts with him to have destroyed all our glory, defence, and happiness.

The first letter I received from him was so remarkable, that some persons of eminent piety, to whom I communicated it, would not be content without copying it out, or making some extracts from it. I persuade myself that my devout reader will not be displeased that I insert the greater part of it here, especially as it serves to illustrate the affectionate sense which he had of the divine goodness in his conversion, though more than twenty years had passed since that memorable event happened. Having already mentioned my ever dear and honoured friend Dr. Isaac Watts, he adds:

"I have been in pain these several years lest that excellent person, that sweet singer in our Israel, should have been called to heaven before I had an opportunity of letting him know how much his works have been blessed to me, and, of course, returning him my hearty thanks; for though it is owing to the operation of the blessed Spirit that any thing works effectually upon our hearts, yet if we are not thankful to the instrument which God is pleased to make use of, whom we do see, how shall we be thankful to the Almighty, whom we have not seen? I desire to bless God for the good news of his recovery, and entreat you to tell him, that although I cannot keep pace with him here in celebrating the high praises of our glorious Redeemer, which is the greatest grief of my heart, yet I am persuaded, that when I join the glorious company above, where there will be no drawbacks, none will outsing me there, because I shall not find any that will be more indebted to the wonderful riches of divine grace than I.

"Give me a place at thy saints' feet,
Or some fallen angel's vacant seat;
I'll strive to sing as loud as they
Who sit above in brighter day.

"I know it is natural for every one who has felt the almighty power which raised our glorious Redeemer from the grave, to believe his case singular; but I have made every one in this respect submit as soon as he has heard my story. And if you seemed so surprised at the account which I gave you, what will you be when you hear it all?

"Oh, if I had an angel's voice,
And could be heard from pole to pole;
I would to all the listening world
Proclaim thy goodness to my soul."

He then concludes, after some expressions of endearment, (which, with whatever pleasure I review them, I must not here insert)—

"If you knew what a natural aversion I have to writing, you would be astonished at the length of this letter, which is, I believe, the longest I ever wrote. But my heart warms when I write to you, which makes my pen move the easier. I hope it will please our gracious God long to preserve you, a blessed instrument in his hand, of doing great good in the church of Christ; and that you may always enjoy a thriving soul in a healthful body, shall be the continual prayer of," &c.

As our intimacy grew, our mutual affection increased; and "my dearest friend" was the form of address with which most of his epistles of the last years were begun and ended. Many of them are filled up with his sentiments of those writings which I published during these years, which he read with great attention, and of which he speaks in terms which it becomes me to suppress, and to impute, in a considerable degree, to the kind prejudices of so endeared a friendship. He gives me repeated assurances "that he was daily mindful of me in his prayers"—a circumstance which I cannot recollect without the greatest thankfulness; and the loss of which I should more deeply lament, did I not hope that the happy effect of these prayers might still continue, and might run into all my remaining days.

It might be a pleasure to me to make several

extracts from many others of his letters; but it is a pleasure which I ought to suppress, and rather to reflect, with unfeigned humility, how unworthy I was of such regards from such a person, and of that divine goodness which gave me such a friend in him. I shall, therefore, only add two general remarks, which offer themselves from several of his letters. The one is, that there is in some of them, as our freedom increased, an agreeable vein of humour and pleasantry, which shows how easy religion sat upon him, and how far he was from placing any part of it in a gloomy melancholy, or stiff formality. The other is, that he frequently refers to domestic circumstances, such as the illness or recovery of my children, &c., which I am surprised how a man of his extensive and important business could so distinctly bear upon his mind. But his memory was good, and his heart was yet better; and his friendship was such, that nothing which sensibly affected the heart of one whom he honoured with it, left his own but slightly touched. I have all imaginable reason to believe that in many instances his prayers were not only offered for us in general terms, but varied as our particular situation required. Many quotations might verify this; but I decline troubling the reader with an enumeration of passages in which it was only the abundance of friendly sympathy that gave this truly great as well as good man so cordial a concern.

After this correspondence, carried on for the space of about three years, and some interviews which we had enjoyed at different places, he came to spend some time with us at Northampton, and brought with him his lady and his two eldest children. I had here an opportunity of taking a much nearer view of his character, and surveying it in a much greater variety of lights than before; and my esteem for him increased in proportion to these opportunities. What I have written with respect to his conduct in relative life, was in a great measure drawn from what I now saw; and I shall mention here some other points in his behaviour which particularly struck my mind, and likewise shall touch on his sentiments on some topics of importance which he freely communicated to me, and which I have remarked on account of that wisdom and propriety which pervaded them.

CHAPTER X.

DEVOTION AND CHARITY.

THERE was nothing more observable in Colonel Gardiner than the exemplary gravity, composure, and reverence with which he attended public worship. Copious as he was in his secret devotions before he engaged in it, he always began them early, so as not to be retarded by them when he should resort to the house of God. He, and all his soldiers who chose to worship with him, were generally there (as I have already hinted) before the service began, that the entrance of so many of them at once might not disturb the congregation already engaged in devotion, and that there might be a better opportunity of bringing the mind to a becoming attention, and preparing it for converse with the Divine Being. While acts of worship were going on, whether of prayer or singing, he always stood up; and whatever regard he might have for persons who passed by m at that time, though it were to come into e same pew, he never paid any compliment to em; and often has he expressed his wonder at e indecorum of breaking off our addresses to od to bow to a fellow-creature, which he thought a much greater indecency than it would be, on a little occasion and circumstance, to interrupt an address to our prince. During the time of preaching, his eye was commonly fixed upon the minister, though sometimes turned round upon the auditory, against whom, if he observed any to trifle, he was filled with just indignation. I have known instances in which, upon making the remark, he has communicated it to some friend of the persons who were guilty of it, that proper application might be made to prevent it for the time to come.

A more devout communicant at the table of the Lord has perhaps seldom been any where known. Often have I had the pleasure to see that manly countenance softened to all the marks of humiliation and contrition on this occasion; and to discern, in spite of all his efforts to conceal them, streams of tears flowing down from his eyes, while he has been directing them to those memorials of his Redeemer's love. Some who have conversed intimately with him after he came from that ordinance, have observed a visible abstraction from surrounding objects, by which there seemed reason to imagine that his soul was wrapped up in holy contemplation. I particularly remember, that when we had once spent a great part of the following Monday in riding together, he made an apology to me for being so absent as he seemed, by telling me "that his heart was flown upwards, before he was aware, to Him 'whom, not having seen, he loved;'* and that he was rejoicing in him with such unspeakable joy, that he could not hold it down to creature converse."

In all the offices of friendship he was remarkably ready, and had a most sweet and engaging manner of performing them, which greatly heightened the obligations he conferred. He seemed not to set any high value upon any benefit he bestowed, but did it without the least parade, as a thing which in those circumstances came of course, where he had professed love and respect; which he was not over forward to do, though he treated strangers, and those who were most his inferiors, very courteously, and always

* This alluded to the subject of the sermon the day before, which was 1 Pet. i. 8.

seemed, because he in truth always was, glad of any opportunity of doing them good.

He was particularly zealous in vindicating the reputation of his friends in their absence; and though I cannot recollect that I had ever an opportunity of immediately observing this, as I do not know that I ever was present with him when any ill was spoken of others at all; yet, by what I have heard him say with relation to attempts to injure the character of worthy and useful men, I have reason to believe that no man living was more sensible of the baseness and infamy, as well as the cruelty, of such conduct. He knew and despised the low principles of resentment for unreasonable expectations disappointed, of personal attachment to men of some crossing interests, of envy, and of party zeal, from whence such a conduct often proceeds; and he was particularly offended when he found it (as he frequently did) in persons that set up for the greatest patrons of liberty, virtue, and candour. He looked upon the murderers of reputation and usefulness as some of the vilest pests of society, and plainly showed on every proper occasion that he thought it the part of a generous, benevolent and courageous man to exert himself in tracing and hunting down the slander, that the authors or abettors of it might be less capable of mischief for the future.

The most plausible objection that I ever heard to Colonel Gardiner's character is, that he was too much attached to some religious principles, established indeed in the churches both of England and Scotland, but which have of late years been much disputed, and from which, it is at least generally supposed, not a few in both have thought proper to depart—whatever expedients they may have found to quiet their consciences, in subscribing those formularies in which they are plainly taught. His zeal was especially apparent in opposition to those doctrines which seemed to derogate from the divine honours of the Son and Spirit of God, and from the freedom of divine grace, of the reality and necessity of its operations in the conversion and salvation of sinners.

With relation to these I must observe, that it was his most steadfast persuasion that all those notions which represent our blessed Redeemer and the Holy Spirit as mere creatures, or which set aside the atonement of the former, or the influences of the latter, sap the very foundation of Christianity by rejecting the most glorious doctrines peculiar to it. He had attentively observed (what indeed is too obvious) the unhappy influence which the denial of these principles often has on the character of ministers, and on their success, and was persuaded that an attempt to substitute that mutilated form of Christianity which remains, when these essentials of it are taken away, has proved one of the most successful methods which the great enemy of souls has ever taken, in these latter days, to lead men by insensible degrees into deism, vice, and perdition. He also sagaciously observed the artful manner in which obnoxious tenets are often maintained or insinuated, with all that mixture of zeal and address with which they are propagated in the world, even by those who had most solemnly professed to believe, and engaged to teach the contrary; and as he really apprehended that the glory of God and the salvation of souls were concerned, his piety and charity made him eager and strenuous in opposing what he judged to be errors of so pernicious a nature. Yet I must declare, that, according to what I have known of him, (and I believe he opened his heart on these topics to me with as much freedom as to any man living,) he was not ready, upon light suspicions, to charge tenets which he thought so pernicious on any, especially where he saw the appearances of a good temper and life, which he always reverenced and loved in persons of all sentiments and professions. He severely condemned causeless jealousies and evil surmisings of every kind, and extended that charity, in this respect, both to clergy and laity, which good Bishop Burnet was so ready, according to his own account, to limit to the latter, "of believing every man good till he knew him to be bad, and his notions right till he knew them wrong." He could not but be very sensible of the unhappy consequences which may follow on attacking the characters of men, especially of those who are ministers of the gospel; and if, through a mixture of human frailty, from which the best of men, in the best of their meanings and intentions, are not entirely free, he had ever, in the warmth of his heart, dropped a word which might be injurious to any on that account, (which I believe very seldom happened,) he would gladly retract it on better information; and this was perfectly agreeable to that honest and generous frankness of temper in which I never knew any man who excelled him.

On the whole, it was indeed his deliberate judgment that the Arian, Socinian, and Pelagian doctrines were highly dishonourable to God, and dangerous to the souls of men; and that it was the duty of private Christians to be greatly on their guard against those ministers by whom they are entertained, lest their minds should be corrupted from the simplicity that is in Christ. Yet he sincerely abhorred the thought of persecution for conscience sake; of the absurdity and iniquity of which, in all its kinds and degrees, he had as deep and rational a conviction as any man. Indeed the generosity of his heroic heart could hardly bear to think that those glorious truths which he so cordially loved, and which he assuredly believed to be capable of such fair support both from reason and the word of God, should be disgraced by methods of defence and propagation common to the most impious and ridiculous falsehoods. Nor did he by any means approve of passionate and furious ways of vindicating the most vital and important doctrines of the gospel; for he knew that to maintain the most benevolent religion in the world by such malevolent and infernal methods was destroying the end to accomplish the means; and that it was as impossible that true Christianity should be supported thus, as it is that a man should long be nourished by eating his own flesh. To display the genuine fruits of Christianity in a good life—to be ready to plead with meekness for the doctrines it teaches, and to labour, by every office of humanity and goodness, to gain upon those who oppose it, were the weapons with which this good soldier of Jesus Christ faithfully fought the battles of the Lord. These weapons will always be victorious in his cause; and they who have recourse to others of a different temper, how strong soever they may seem, and how sharp soever they may really be, will find them break in their hands when they exert them most furiously, and are much more likely to wound themselves than to conquer the enemies whom they oppose.

But while I am speaking of Colonel Gardiner's charity in this respect, I must not omit that of another kind, which has indeed engrossed the name of charity, excellent as it is, much more than it ought—I mean almsgiving, for which he was very remarkable. I have often wondered how he was able to do so many generous things in this way. But his frugality fed the spring. He made no pleasurable expense on himself, and was contented with a very decent appearance in his family, without affecting such an air of grandeur as could not have been supported without sacrificing to it satisfactions far nobler, and, to a temper like his, far more delightful. The lively and tender feelings of his heart in favour of the distressed and afflicted made it a self-indulgence to relieve them; and the deep conviction he had of the vain and transitory nature of the enjoyments of this world, together with the sublime view he had of another, engaged him to dispense his bounties with a very liberal hand, and even to seek out proper objects of them. Above all, his sincere and ardent love to the Lord Jesus Christ engaged him to feel, with a true sympathy, the concerns of his poor members. In consequence of this, he honoured several of his friends with commissions for the relief of the poor; and particularly, with relation to some under my pastoral care, he referred it to my discretion to supply them with what I should judge expedient, and frequently pressed me, in his letters, "to be sure not to let them want." And where persons standing in need of his charity happened, as they often did, to be persons of remarkably religious dispositions, it was easy to perceive that he not only loved but honoured them, and really esteemed it an honour which Providence conferred upon him, that he should be made, as it were, the almoner of God for their relief.

I cannot forbear relating a little story here, which, when the colonel himself heard it, gave him such exquisite pleasure, that I hope it will be acceptable to several of my readers. There was in a village about nine miles from Northampton, and in a family which, of all others near me, was afterwards most indebted to him, (though he had never then seen any member of it,) an aged and poor, but eminently good woman, who had, with great difficulty, in the exercise of much faith and patience, diligence and humility, made shift to educate a large family of children after the death of her husband, without being chargeable to the parish; which, as it was quite beyond her hope, she often spoke of with great delight. At length, when worn out with age and infirmities, she lay upon her death-bed, she, in a most lively and affecting manner, expressed her hope and joy in the views of approaching glory. Yet, amidst all the triumphs of such a prospect, there was one remaining care and distress which lay heavy on her mind; this was, that as her journey and her stock of provisions were both ended together, she feared that she must either be buried at the parish expense, or leave to her most dutiful and affectionate daughters the house stripped of some of the few movables which remained in it, in order to perform the last office of duty to her, which she had reason to believe they would do. While she was combatting with this only remaining anxiety, I happened, though I knew not the extremity of her illness, to come in, and to bring with me a guinea which the generous colonel had sent by a special message, on hearing the character of the family, for its relief. A present like this, (probably the most considerable they had ever received in their lives,) coming in this manner from an entire stranger at such a crisis of time, threw my dying friend (for such, amidst all her poverty, I rejoiced to call her) into a perfect transport of joy. She esteemed it a singular favour of Providence sent to her in her last moments as a token for good, and greeted it as a special mark of that loving kindness of God which should attend her for ever. She insisted, therefore, to be raised up in her bed, that she might bless God for it upon her knees, and with her last breath pray for her kind and generous benefactor, and for him who had been the instrument of directing his bounty into this channel. After this she soon expired, and with such tranquillity and sweetness as could not but most sensibly delight all who beheld her, and occasioned many who knew the circumstance to glorify God on her behalf.

The colonel's last residence at Northampton was in June and July 1742, when Lord Cadogan's regiment of dragoons was quartered here. Here I cannot but observe, that wherever that regiment came, it was remarkable not only for the fine appearance it made, and for the exactness with which it performed its various exercises, (of which it had about this time the honour to receive the most illustrious testimonials,) but also for the great sobriety and regularity of the soldiers. Many of the officers copied after the excellent pattern which they had daily before their eyes; and a considerable number of the private men seemed to be persons not only of strict virtue, but of serious piety. I doubt not but they found their abundant account in it, not only in the serenity and happiness of their own minds, which is beyond comparison the most important consideration; but also, in some degree, in the obliging and respectful treatment which they generally met with in their quarters. I mention this, because I am persuaded that if gentlemen of their profession knew, and would reflect, how much more comfortable they make their own quarters by a sober, orderly, and obliging conduct, they would be regular out of mere self-love, if they were not influenced, as I heartily wish they may always be, by a nobler principle.

CHAPTER XI.

EMBARKS FOR FLANDERS.

TOWARDS the latter end of this year he embarked for Flanders, and spent some considerable time with the regiment at Ghent, where he much regretted the want of those religious ordinances and opportunities which had made his other abodes delightful. But as he had made so eminent a progress in that divine life which they are all intended to promote, he could not be inactive in the cause of God. I have now before me a letter, dated from thence October 16, 1742, in which he writes:

"As for me, I am indeed in a dry and barren land, where no water is. Rivers of waters run down mine eyes, because nothing is to be heard in our Sodom but blaspheming the name of my God, and I not honoured as the instrument of doing any great service. It is true, I have reformed six or seven field-officers of swearing. I dine every day with them, and have entered them into a voluntary contract to pay a shilling to the poor for every oath, and it is wonderful to observe the effect it has had already. One of them told me this day at dinner that it had really such an influence upon him, that being at cards last night when another officer fell a swearing, he was not able to bear it, but rose up and left the company. So you see, restraints at first arising from a low principle may improve into something better."

During his abode here, he had a great deal of business upon his hands, and had also, in some marches, the care of more regiments than his own; and it has been very delightful to me to observe what a degree of converse with heaven, and the God of it, he maintained amidst these scenes of hurry and fatigue, of which the reader may find a remarkable specimen in the following letter, dated from Lichwick in the beginning of April 1743, which was one of the last I received from him while abroad. It begins with these words:—

"Yesterday being the Lord's day, at six in the morning I had the pleasure of receiving yours at Nortonick; and it proved a Sabbath day's blessing to me. Some time before it reached me," (from whence, by the way, it may be observed that his former custom of rising so early in his devotions was still retained,) "I had been wrestling with God with many tears; and when I had read it, I returned to my knees again to give hearty thanks to him for all his goodness to you and yours, and also to myself, in that he hath been pleased to stir up so many who are dear to him, to be mindful of me at the throne of grace."

Then, after the mention of some other particulars, he adds:—

"Blessed and adored for ever be the holy name of my Heavenly Father, who holds my soul in life, and my body in perfect health! Were I to recount his mercy and goodness to me even in the midst of all these hurries, I should never have done. I hope your Master will still encourage you in his work, and make you a blessing to many. My dearest friend, I am much more yours than I can express, and shall remain so while I am J. G."

In this correspondence I had a further opportunity of discovering that humble resignation to the will of God which made so amiable a part of his character, and of which I had before seen so many instances. He speaks, in the letter from which I have just been giving an extract, of the hope he had expressed in a former of seeing us again that winter; and he adds:—

"To be sure, it would have been a great pleasure to me; but we poor mortals form projects, and the Almighty ruler of the universe disposes of all as he pleases. A great many of us were getting ready for our return to England, when we received an order to march towards Frankfort, to the great surprise of the whole army, neither can any of us comprehend what we are to do there; for there is no enemy in that country, the French army being marched into Bavaria, where I am sure we cannot follow them. But it is the will of the Lord, and his will be done! I desire to bless and praise my Heavenly Father that I am entirely resigned to it. It is no matter where I go, or what becomes of me, so that God may be glorified in my life, or my death. I should rejoice much to hear that all my friends were equally resigned."

The mention of this article reminds me of another relating to the views which he had of obtaining a regiment for himself. He endeavoured to deserve it by the most faithful services; some of them, indeed, beyond what the strength of his constitution could well bear—for the weather in some of these marches proved exceedingly bad, and yet he would be always at the head of his people, that he might look, with the exactest care, to every thing that concerned them. This obliged him to neglect the beginnings of a feverish illness, the natural consequence of which was that it grew very formidable, forced a long confinement upon him, and gave animal nature a shock which it never recovered.

In the mean time, as he had the promise of a regiment before he quitted England, his friends were continually expecting an occasion of congratulating him on having received the command of one. Still they were disappointed, and on some of them the disappointment seemed to sit heavy. As for the colonel himself, he seemed quite easy about it, and appeared much greater in that easy situation of mind than the highest military honours and preferments could have made him. With great pleasure do I at this moment recollect the unaffected serenity, and even indifference, with which he expresses himself upon this occasion, in a letter to me, dated about the beginning of April, 1743.

"The disappointment of a regiment is nothing to me, for I am satisfied that, had it been for God's glory, I should have had it, and I should have been sorry to have had it on any other terms. My Heavenly Father has bestowed upon me infinitely more than if he had made me emperor of the whole world."

I find several parallel expressions in other letters, and those to his lady about the same time were just in the same strain. In an extract from one which was written from Aix-la-Chapelle, April 21, the same year, I meet with these words:

"People here imagine I must be sadly troubled that I have not got a regiment, (for six out of seven vacant are now disposed of): but they are strangely mistaken, for it has given me no sort of trouble. My Heavenly Father knows what is best for me; and blessed and ever adored be his name, he has given me an entire resignation to his will. Besides, I do not know that I met with any disappointment, since I was a Christian, but it pleased God to discover to me that it was plainly for my advantage, by bestowing something better upon me afterwards, many instances of which I am able to produce; and therefore I should be the greatest of monsters, if I did not trust in him."

I should be guilty of a great omission, if I were not to add how remarkably the event corresponded with his faith on this occasion; for whereas he had no intimation or expectation of any thing more than a regiment of foot, his Majesty was pleased, out of his great goodness, to give him a regiment of dragoons which was then quartered in his own neighborhood. It is properly remarked by the reverend and worthy person through whose hand this letter was transmitted to me, that when the colonel thus expressed himself, he could have no prospect of what he afterwards so soon obtained, as General Bland's regiment, to which he was advanced, was only vacant on the 19th of April—that is, two days before the date of this letter, when it was impossible he should have any notice of that vacancy. It also deserves observation, that some few days after the colonel was thus unexpectedly promoted to the command of these dragoons, Lord Cornwallis's regiment of foot, then in Flanders, became vacant. Now, had this happened before his promotion to General Bland's, Colonel Gardiner, in all probability, would only have had that regiment of foot, and so would have continued in Flanders. When the affair was settled, he informs Lady Frances of it in a letter dated from a village near Frankfort, 3d May, in which he refers to his former of the 21st of April, observing how remarkably it was verified "in God's having given him" (for so he expresses it, agreeably to the views which he continually maintained of the universal agency of Divine Providence) "what he had no expectation of, and what was so much better than that which he had missed—a regiment of dragoons quartered at his own door."

CHAPTER XII.

RETURN TO ENGLAND.

It appeared to him that by this remarkable event Providence called him home. Accordingly, though he had other preferments offered him in the army, he chose to return, and I believe the more willingly, as he did not expect there would have been an action. Just at this time it pleased God to give him an awful instance of the uncertainty of human prospects and enjoyments, by that violent fever which seized him at Ghent on his way to England, and perhaps the more severely for the efforts he made to push on his journey, though he had for some days been much indisposed. It was, I think, one of the first fits of severe illness he had ever met with, and he was ready to look upon it as a sudden call into eternity; but it gave him no painful alarm in that view. He committed himself to the God of his life, and in a few weeks he was so well recovered as to be capable of pursuing his journey, though not without difficulty. I cannot but think it might have conduced much to a more perfect recovery than he ever attained, to have allowed himself a longer repose, in order to recruit his exhausted strength and spirits. But there was an activity in his temper not easy to be restrained, and it was now stimulated, not only with a desire to see his friends, but of being with his regiment, that he might omit nothing in his power to regulate their morals and their discipline, and to form them for public service. Accordingly, about the middle of June, 1743, he passed through London, where he had the honour of waiting on their royal highnesses, the Prince and Princess of Wales, and of receiving from both the most obliging token of favour and esteem. He arrived at Northampton on Monday the 21st of June, and spent part of three days there. But the great pleasure which his return and preferment gave us, was much abated by observing his countenance so sadly altered, and the many marks of languor and remaining disorder which evidently appeared, so that he really looked ten years older than he had done ten months before. I had, however, a satisfaction sufficient to counterbalance much of the concern which this alteration gave me, in a renewed opportunity of observing, indeed more sensibly than ever, in how remarkable a degree he was dead to the enjoyments and views of this mortal life. When I congratulated him on the favourable appearances of Providence for him in the late event, he briefly told me the remarkable circumstances that attended it, with the most genuine expressions of gratitude to God for them; but added, "that as his account was increased with his income, power, influence, and his cares were proportionably increased too, it was, as to his own personal concern, much the same to him whether he had remained in his former station, or been elevated to this; but that if God should by this means honour him as an instrument of doing more good than he could otherwise have done, he should rejoice in it."

I perceived that the near views he had taken of eternity, in the illness from which he was then so imperfectly recovered, had not in the least alarmed him; but that he would have been entirely willing, had such been the determination of God, to have been cut short in a foreign land, without any earthly friend near him, and in the midst of a journey undertaken with hopes and prospects so pleasing to nature, which appeared to me no inconsiderable evidence of the strength of his faith. But we shall wonder the less at this extraordinary resignation, if we consider the joyful and assured prospect which he had of a happiness infinitely superior beyond the grave; of which that worthy minister of the church of Scotland, who had an opportunity of conversing with him quickly after his return, and having the memorable story of his conversion from his own mouth, (as I have hinted above,) writes thus in his letter to me, dated Jan. 14, 1746–7:

"When he came to review his regiment at Linlithgow, in summer 1743, after having given me the wonderful story as above, he concluded in words to this purpose: Let me die whenever it shall please God, or wherever it shall be, I am sure I shall go to the mansions of eternal glory, and enjoy my God and my Redeemer in heaven for ever."

While he was with us at this time he appeared deeply affected with the sad state of things as to religion and morals, and seemed to apprehend that the rod of God was hanging over so sinful a nation. He observed a great deal of disaffection which the enemies of the government had, by a variety of artifices, been raising in Scotland for some years; and the number of Jacobites there, together with the defenceless state in which our island then was, with respect to the number of its forces at home, (of which he spoke at once with great concern and astonishment,) led him to expect an invasion from France, and an attempt in favour of the Pretender, much sooner than it happened. I have heard him often say, many years before it came so near being accomplished, "that a few thousands might have a fair chance for marching from Edinburgh to London uncontrolled, and throw the whole kingdom into an astonishment" And I have great reason to believe that this was one main consideration which engaged him to make such haste to his regiment, then quartered in those parts, as he imagined there was not a spot of ground where he might be more likely to have a call to expose his life in the service of his country, and perhaps, by appearing on a proper call early in its defence, be instrumental in suppressing the beginnings of most formidable mischief. How rightly he judged in these things, the event too evidently showed.

The evening before our last separation, as I knew I could not more agreeably entertain the valuable friend who was then my guest, I preached a sermon in my own house, with some peculiar reference to his case and circumstances, from those ever-memorable words, than which I have never felt any more powerful and more comfortable: Psalm xci. 14, 15, 16, "Because he hath set his love upon me, therefore will I deliver him: I will set him on high, because he hath known my name. He shall call upon me, and I will answer him; I will be with him in trouble, I will deliver him, and honour him: with long life (or length of days) will I satisfy him, and show him my salvation." This scripture could not but lead our meditations to survey the character of the good man, as one who so knows the name of the blessed God—has such a deep apprehension of the glories and perfections of his nature—as determinately to set his love upon him, to make him the supreme object of his most ardent and constant affection. And it suggested the most sublime and animating hopes to persons of such a character, that their prayers shall be always acceptable to God; that though they may, and must, be called to their share in the troubles and calamities of life, yet they may assure themselves of the divine presence in all, which will issue in their deliverance, in their exaltation, sometimes in distinguished honour and esteem among men, and, it may be, in a long course of useful and happy years on earth; at least, which shall undoubtedly end in seeing, to their perpetual delight, the complete salvation of God, in a world where they shall enjoy length of days for ever and ever, and employ them all in adoring the great Author of their salvation and felicity. It is evident that these natural thoughts on such a Scripture were matters of universal concern. Yet had I, as a minister of the gospel, known that this was the last time I should address Colonel Gardiner, and had I foreseen the scenes through which God was about to lead him, I hardly know what considerations I could have suggested with more peculiar propriety. The attention, elevation, and delight with which he heard them, were very apparent, and the pleasure which the observation of it gave me continues to this moment.

Let me be permitted to digress so far as to add, that this is indeed the great support of a Christian minister under the many discouragements and disappointments which he meets with in his attempts to fix upon the profligate or the thoughtless part of mankind a deep sense of religious truth; that there is another important part of his work in which he may hope to be more generally successful; as, by plain, artless, but serious discourses, the great principles of Christian duty and hope may be nourished and invigorated in good men, their graces watered as at the root, and their souls animated, both to persevere and improve in holiness. When we are effectually performing such benevolent offices, so well suiting our immortal natures, to persons whose hearts are cemented with ours in the bonds of the most endearing and sacred friendship, it is too little to say that it overpays the fatigue of our labours; it even swallows up all sense of it in the most rational and sublime pleasure.

An incident occurred that evening, which, at least for the oddness of it, may deserve a place in these memoirs. I had then with me one Thomas Porter, a poor but very honest and religious man, (now living at Hatfield Broad-Oak in Essex,) who is quite unacquainted with letters, so as not to be able to distinguish one from another, yet is master of the contents of the Bible in so extraordinary a degree, that he has not only fixed an immense number of texts in his memory, but, merely by hearing them quoted in sermons, has registered there the chapter and verse in which these passages are to be found. This is attended with a marvellous facility in directing readers to turn to them, and a most unaccountable talent of fixing on such as suit almost every imaginable variety of circumstances in common life. There are in this case two considerations that make it the more wonderful;—the one, that he is a person of very low genius, having, besides a stammering which makes his speech almost unintelligible to strangers, so wild and awkward a manner of behaviour, that he is frequently taken for an idiot, and seems in many things to be indeed so;—the other, that he grew up to manhood in a very licentious course of living, and an entire ignorance of divine things, so that all these exact impressions on his memory have been made in his riper years. I thought it would not be disagreeable to the colonel to introduce to him this odd phenomenon, which many hundreds of people have had a curiosity to examine; and, among all the strange things I have seen in him, I never remember any that equalled what passed on this occasion. On hearing the colonel's profession, and receiving some hints of his religious character, he ran through a vast variety of scriptures, beginning at the Pentateuch and going on to the Revelation, relating either to the dependence to be fixed on God for the success of military preparations, or to the instances and promises occurring there for his care of good men in the most imminent dangers, or to the encouragement to despise perils and death, while engaged in a good cause, and supported by the views of a happy immortality. I believe he quoted more than twenty of these passages, and I must freely own that I know not who could have chosen them with greater propriety. If my memory deceive me not, the last of this catalogue was that from which I afterwards preached, on the lamented occasion of this great man's fall: "Be thou faithful unto death, and I will give thee a crown of life." We were all astonished at so remarkable a fact, and I question not but many of my readers will think the memory of it worthy of being thus preserved.

But to return to my main subject: The day after the sermon and conversation of which I have been speaking, I took my last leave of my inestimable friend, after attending him some part of his way northward. The first stage of our journey was to the cottage of that poor but religious family which I had before occasion to mention as relieved, and indeed in a great measure subsisted by his charity. Nothing could be more delightful than to observe the condescension with which he conversed with these his humble pensioners. We there put up our last united prayers together; and he afterwards expressed, in the strongest terms I have ever heard him use on such an occasion, the singular pleasure with which he had joined in them. Indeed it was no small satisfaction to me to have an opportunity of recommending such a valuable friend to the divine protection and blessing, with that particular freedom and enlargement on what was peculiar in his circumstances, which hardly any other situation, unless we had been quite alone, could so conveniently have admitted. We went from thence to the table of a person of distinction in the neighbourhood, where he had an opportunity of showing in how decent and graceful a manner he could unite the Christian and the gentleman, and give conversation an improving and religious turn, without violating any of the rules of polite behaviour, or saying or doing any thing which looked at all constrained or affected. Here we took our last embrace, committing each other to the care of the God of heaven; and the colonel pursued his journey to the north, where he spent the remainder of his days.

The more I reflect upon this appointment of Providence, the more I discern the beauty and wisdom of it—not only as it led directly to that glorious period of life with which God had determined to honour him, and in which, I think, it becomes all his friends to rejoice, but also as the retirement on which he entered could not but have a happy tendency to favour his more immediate and complete preparation for so speedy a remove. To this we may add, that it must probably have a very powerful influence to promote the interests of religion (incomparably the greatest of all interests) among the members of his own family, who must surely be edified by such daily lessons as they received from his lips, when they saw them illustrated and enforced by so admirable an example, and for two complete years. It is the more remarkable, as I cannot find from the memoirs of his life in my hands that he had ever been so long at home since he had a family, or indeed, from his childhood, ever so long at a time in any one place.

With how clear a lustre his lamp shone, and with what holy vigour his loins were girded up in the service of his God in these his latter days, I learn in part from the letters of several excellent persons in the ministry, or in secular life, with whom I have since conversed or corresponded. In his many letters dated from Bankton during this period, I have still further evidence how happy he was amidst those infirmities of body, which his tenderness for me would seldom allow him to mention; for it appears from them what a daily intercourse he kept up with Heaven, and what delightful communion with God crowned his attendance on public ordinances, and his sweet hours of devout retirement. He mentions his sacramental opportunities with peculiar relish, crying out, as in a holy rapture, in reference to one and another of them, "Oh how gracious a Master do we serve! how pleasant is his service; how rich the entertainments of his love! yet how poor and cold are our services!" But I will not multiply quotations of this sort after those I have given above, which may be a sufficient specimen of many more in the same strain. This hint may suffice to show that the same ardour of soul held out in a great measure to the last; and indeed it seems that towards the close of life, like the flame of a lamp almost expiring, it sometimes exerted an unusual blaze.

He spent much of his time at Bankton in religious solitude; and one most intimately conversant with him assures me that the traces of that delightful converse with God which he enjoyed in it might easily be discerned in the solemn yet cheerful countenance with which he often came out of his closet. Yet his exercises there must sometimes have been very mournful, considering the melancholy views which he had of the state of our public affairs.

"I should be glad," says he, (in a letter which he sent me about the close of the year 1743,) "to hear what wise and good people among you think of the present circumstances of things. For my own part, though I thank God I fear nothing for myself, my apprehensions for the public are very gloomy, considering the deplorable prevalency of almost all kinds of wickedness amongst us—the natural consequence of the contempt of the gospel. I am daily offering my prayers to God for this sinful land of ours, over which his judgments seem to be gathering; and my strength is sometimes so exhausted with those strong cries and tears, which I pour out before God on this occasion, that I am hardly able to stand when I arise from my knees."

If we have many remaining to stand in the breach with equal fervency, I hope, crying as our provocations are, that God will still be entreated for us, and save us.

Most of the other letters I had the pleasure of receiving from him after our last separation, are either filled, like those of former years, with tender expressions of affectionate solicitude for my domestic comfort and public usefulness, or relate to the writings I published during this time, or to the affairs of his eldest son, then under my care. But these are things which are by no means of a nature to be communicated here. It is enough to remark, in general, that the Christian was still mingled with all the care of the friend and the parent.

CHAPTER XIII.

REVIVAL OF RELIGION.

BUT I think it incumbent upon me to observe, that during this time, and for some preceding years, his attention, ever wakeful to such concerns, was much engaged by some religious appearances which happened about this time both in England and Scotland, and with regard to which some may be curious to know the colonel's sentiments. He communicated them to me with the most unreserved freedom; and I cannot apprehend myself under any engagement to conceal them, as I am persuaded that it will be no prejudice to his memory that they should be publicly known.

It was from Colonel Gardiner's pen that I received the first notice of that ever-memorable scene which was opened at Kilsyth, under the ministry of the Rev. Mr. M'Culloch, in the month of February, 1741–2. He communicated to me the copy of two letters from that eminently-favoured servant of God, giving an account of that extraordinary success which had within a few days accompanied his preaching, when, as I remember, in a little more than a fortnight, one hundred and thirty souls, who had before continued in long insensibility under the faithful preaching of the gospel, were awakened on a sudden to attend to it, as if it had been a new revelation brought down from heaven, and attested by as astonishing miracles as ever were wrought by Peter or Paul, though they only heard it from a person under whose ministry they had sat for several years. Struck with a power and majesty in the word of God which they had never felt before, they crowded his house night and day, making their applications to him for spiritual direction and assistance, with an earnestness and solicitude which floods of tears and cries, that swallowed up their own words and his, could not sufficiently express. The colonel mentioned this at first to me "as matter of eternal praise, which he knew would rejoice my very soul;" and when he saw it spread in the neighbouring parts, and observed the glorious reformation which it produced in the lives of great multitudes, and the abiding fruits of it for succeeding months and years, it increased and confirmed his joy. But the facts relating to this matter have been laid before the world in so authentic a manner, and the agency of divine grace in them has been so rationally vindicated, and so pathetically represented, in what the reverend and judicious Mr. Webster has written upon that subject, that it is altogether superfluous for me to add any thing further than my hearty prayers that the work may be as extensive as it was glorious and divine.*

It was with great pleasure that he received any intelligence of a like kind from England, whether the clergy of the Established Church or dissenting ministers, whether our own countrymen or foreigners, were the instruments of it. Whatever weaknesses or errors might mingle themselves with valuable qualities in such as were active in such a work, he appeared to love and honour them in proportion to the degree he saw reason to believe that their hearts were devoted to the service of Christ, and their attempts owned and succeeded by him. I remember, that mentioning one of

* See "Revivals in Scotland," published by the Board of Publication.

these gentlemen who had been remarkably successful in his ministry, and who seemed to have met with some very unkind usage, he says, "I had rather be that despised, persecuted man, to be an instrument in the hand of the Spirit in converting so many souls, and building up so many in their holy faith, than I would be emperor of the whole world." Yet this steady and judicious Christian, (for such he most assuredly was,) at the same time that he esteemed a man for his good intentions, and his worthy qualities, did not suffer himself to be hurried away into all the singularity of his sentiments, or to admire his imprudences or excesses. On the contrary, he saw and lamented that artifice which the great father of fraud has so long and so successfully been practising, and who, like the enemies of Israel, when he cannot entirely prevent the building of God's temple, does, as it were, offer his assistance to carry on the work, that he may thereby get the most effectual opportunities of obstructing it. The colonel often expressed his astonishment at the wide extremes into which some whom on the whole he thought very worthy men, were permitted to run in many doctrinal and speculative points, and discerned how evidently it appeared from hence that we cannot argue the truth of any doctrine from the success of the preacher, since this would be a kind of demonstration which might equally prove both parts of a contradiction. Yet when he observed that a high regard to the atonement and righteousness of Christ, and to the free grace of God in him, exerted by the operation of the Divine Spirit, was generally common to all who had been peculiarly successful in the conversion and reformation of men, (how widely soever their judgments might differ in other points, and how warmly soever their judgments might oppose each other in consequence of that diversity,) it tended greatly to confirm his faith in these principles, as well as to open his heart in love to all, of every denomination, who maintained an affectionate regard to them. Although what he remarked as to the conduct and success of ministers of the most opposite strains of preaching confirmed him in these sentiments, yet he always esteemed and loved virtuous and benevolent men, even where he thought them the most mistaken in the notions they formed of religion, or in the methods by which they attempted to serve it.

While I thus represent what all who knew him must soon have observed of Colonel Gardiner's affectionate regard to these peculiar doctrines of our holy religion, it is necessary that I should also inform my reader that it was not his opinion that the attention of ministers or their hearers should be wholly engrossed by these, excellent as they are; but that all the parts of the scheme of truth and duty should be regarded in their due connection and proportion. Far from that distempered taste which can bear nothing but cordials, it was his deliberate judgment that the law as well as the gospel should be preached; and hardly any thing gave him greater offence than the irreverent manner in which some who have been ignorantly extolled as the most zealous evangelical preachers, have sometimes been tempted to speak of the former, much indeed to the scandal of all consistent and judicious Christians. He delighted to be instructed in his duty, and to hear much of the inward exercises of the spiritual and divine life. He always wished, so far as I could observe, to have these topics treated in a rational as well as spiritual manner, with solidity and order of thought, with perspicuity and weight of expression, well knowing that religion is a most reasonable service—that God has not chosen idiots or lunatics as the instruments, or nonsense as the means of building up his church—and that though the charge of enthusiasm is often fixed on Christianity and its ministers in a wild, undeserved, and, indeed, on the whole, enthusiastical manner, by some of the loudest or most solemn pretenders to reason, yet there is really such a thing as enthusiasm, against which it becomes the true friends of revelation to be diligently on their guard, lest Christianity, instead of being exalted, should be greatly corrupted and debased, and all manner of absurdity, both in doctrine and practice, introduced by methods which, like persecution, throw truth and falsehood on a level, and render the grossest errors at once more plausible and more incurable. He had too much candour and equity to fix general charges of this nature; but he was really (and I think not vainly,) apprehensive that the emissaries and agents of the most corrupt church that ever dishonoured the Christian name, (by which, it will easily be understood, I mean that of Rome,) might very possibly insinuate themselves into societies to which they could not otherwise have access, and make their advantage of that total resignation of the understanding, and contempt of reason and learning, which nothing but ignorance, delirium, or knavery can dictate, to lead men blindfolded whither it pleased, till it set them down at the foot of an altar where transubstantiation itself was consecrated.

I know not where I can more properly introduce another part of the colonel's character, which, obvious as it was, I have not yet touched upon; I mean his tenderness to those who were under any spiritual distress, wherein he was indeed an example to ministers in a duty more peculiarly theirs. I have seen many amiable instances of this myself, and I have been informed of many others. One of these happened about the time of that awakening in the western parts of Scotland, which I touched upon above, when the Rev. Mr. M'Laurin, of Glasgow, found occasion to witness to the great propriety, judgment, and felicity of manner, with which he addressed spiritual consolation to an afflicted soul who applied to the professor at a time when he had not an opportunity immediately to give audience to the case. Indeed so long ago as the year 1726, I find him writing in this regard to a friend in a strain of tenderness which might well have become the most affectionate and experienced pastor. He there congratulates him on some religious enjoyments lately received, (in part, it seems, by his means) when, among others, he has this modest expression: "If I have been made any way the means of doing you good, give the whole glory to God; for he has been willing to show that the power was entirely of himself, since he has been pleased to make use of so very weak an instrument." In the same letter he admonishes his friend that he should not be too much surprised, if after having been (as he expresses it) upon the mount, he should be brought into the valley again, reminding him that "we live by faith, and not by sensible assurance," and representing that there are some such full communications from God as seem almost to swallow up the actings of faith, from whence they take their rise: "Whereas, when a Christian who walks in darkness, and sees no light, will yet hang, as it were, on the report of an absent Jesus, and" (as one expresses it in allusion to the story of Jacob and Joseph) "can put himself as on the chariot of the promises, to be borne on to Him whom he sees not; there may be sublimer and more acceptable actings of a pure and strong faith than in moments which afford the soul a much more rapturous delight." This is the substance of what he says in this excellent letter. Some of the phrases made use of might not perhaps be intelligible to several of my readers, for which reason I do not exactly transcribe them all; but this is plainly and fully his meaning, and most of the words are his own. The sentiment is surely very just and important; and happy would it be for many excellent persons, who, through wrong notions of the nature of faith, (which was never more misrepresented than now among some,) are perplexing themselves with the most groundless doubts and scruples, if it were more generally understood, admitted, and considered.

CHAPTER XIV.

APPREHENSIONS OF DEATH.

An endeared friend, who was most intimately conversant with the colonel during the last two years of his life, has favoured me with an account of some little circumstances relating to him, which I esteem as precious fragments, by which the consistent tenor of his character may be further illustrated. I shall therefore insert them here, without being very solicitous as to the order in which they are introduced.

He perceived himself evidently in a very declining state from his first arrival in Britain, and seemed to entertain a fixed apprehension that he should continue but a little while longer in life. "He expected death," says my good correspondent, "and was delighted with the prospect," which did not grow less amiable by a nearer approach. The word of God, with which he had as intimate an acquaintance as most men I ever knew, and on which (especially on the New Testament) I have heard him make many very judicious and accurate remarks, was still his daily study; and it furnished him with matter of frequent conversation, much to the edification and comfort of those that were about him. It was recollected that, among other passages, he had lately spoken of the following as having made a deep impression on his mind: "My soul, wait thou only upon God!" He would repeat it again and again, *only, only, only!* So plainly did he see, and so deeply did he feel, the vanity of creature confidence and expectations. With the strongest attestation would he often mention those words in Isaiah, as verified by long experience: "Thou wilt keep him in perfect peace, whose mind is stayed on thee, because he trusteth in thee." And with peculiar satisfaction would he utter those heroic words in Habakkuk, which he found armour of proof against every fear and every contingency: "Though the fig tree shall not blossom, neither shall fruit be in the vines; the labour of the olive shall fail, and the fields shall yield no meat; the flocks shall be cut off from the fold, and there shall be no herd in the stalls; yet I will rejoice in the Lord, I will joy in the God of my salvation." The 145th Psalm was also spoken of by him with great delight, and Dr. Watts's version of it, as well as several others of that excellent person's poetical compositions. My friend who transmits to me this account, adds the following words, which I desire to insert with the deepest sentiments of unfeigned humility and self-abasement before God, as most unworthy the honour of contributing in the least degree to the joys and graces of one so much my superior in every part of the Christian character. "As the joy with which good men see the happy fruits of their labours, makes a part of the present reward of the servants of God and the friends of Jesus, it must not be omitted, even in a letter to you, that your spiritual hymns were among his most delightful and soul-improving repasts, particularly those on beholding transgressors with grief, and Christ's Message." What is added concerning my book of the Rise and Progress of Religion, and the terms in which he expressed his esteem of it, I cannot suffer to pass my pen; only I desire most sincerely to bless God, that, especially by the last chapters of that treatise, I had an opportunity, at so great a distance, of exhibiting some offices of Christian friendship to this excellent person in the closing scenes of life, which it would have been my greatest joy to have performed in person, had Providence permitted me then to have been near him.

The former of these hymns, which my correspondent mentions as having been so agreeable to Colonel Gardiner, I have given the reader already. The latter, which is called Christ's Message, took its rise from Luke iv. 18, 19, and is as follows:

Hark! the glad sound! the Saviour comes
The Saviour promised long!
Let every heart prepare a throne,
And every voice a song.

On him the Spirit, largely poured,
Exerts its sacred fire:
Wisdom and might, and zeal and love,
His holy breast inspire.

He comes the prisoners to release,
In Satan's bondage held;
The gates of brass before him burst,
The iron fetters yield.

He comes, from thickest films of vice
To clear the mental ray,
And on the eye-balls of the blind
To pour celestial day.*

* This stanza is mostly borrowed from Mr. Pope.

He comes the broken heart to bind;
  The bleeding soul to cure;
And with the treasures of his grace
  To enrich the humble poor.

His silver trumpets publish loud
  The jubilee of the Lord;
Our debts are all remitted now,
  Our heritage restored.

Our glad hosannas, Prince of Peace!
  Thy welcome shall proclaim;
And heaven's eternal arches ring
  With thy beloved name.

There is one hymn more I shall beg leave to add, plain as it is, which Colonel Gardiner has been heard to mention with particular regard, as expressing the inmost sentiments of his soul, and they were undoubtedly so in the last rational moments of his expiring life. It is called 'Christ precious to the Believer,' and was composed to be sung after a sermon on 1 Pet. ii. 7.

Jesus! I love thy charming name,
  'Tis music to my ear:
Fain would I sound it out so loud,
  That earth and heaven should hear.

Yes! thou art precious to my soul,
  My transport and my trust:
Jewels to thee are gaudy toys,
  And gold is sordid dust.

All my capacious powers can wish,
  In thee most richly meet;

Nor to my eyes is life so dear,
  Nor friendship half so sweet.

Thy grace still dwells upon my heart,
  And sheds its fragrance there;
The noblest balm of all its wounds,
  The cordial of its care.

I'll speak the honours of thy name
  With my last labouring breath;
Then speechless clasp thee in my arms,
  The antidote of death.

Those who were intimate with Colonel Gardiner, must have observed how ready he was to give a devotional turn to any subject that occurred. In particular, the spiritual and heavenly disposition of his soul discovered itself in the reflections and improvements which he made when reading history, in which he took a great deal of pleasure, as persons remarkable for their knowledge of mankind, and observation of Providence, generally do. I have an instance of this before me, which, though too natural to be at all surprising, will, I dare say, be pleasing to the devout mind. He had just been reading, in Rollin's extracts from Xenophon, the answer which the lady of Tigranes made when all the company were extolling Cyrus, and expressing the admiration with which his appearance and behaviour struck them. The question being asked her, What she thought of him? she answered, "I do not know; I did not observe him." On what, then, said one of the company, did you fix your attention? "On him," replied she, (referring to the generous speech which her husband had just made,) "who said he would give a thousand lives to ransom my liberty." "Oh," cried the colonel, when reading it, "how ought we to fix our eyes and hearts on Him who, not in offer, but in reality, gave his own precious life to ransom us from the most dreadful slavery, and from eternal destruction!" But this is only one instance among a thousand. His heart was so habitually set upon divine things, and he had such a permanent and overflowing sense of the love of Christ, that he could not forbear connecting such reflections with a multitude of more distant occasions occurring in daily life, on which less advanced Christians would not have thought of them; and thus, like our great Master, he made every little incident a source of devotion, and an instrument of holy zeal.

Enfeebled as his constitution was, he was still intent on improving his time to some valuable purpose; and when his friends expostulated with him that he gave his body so little rest, he used to answer, "It will rest long enough in the grave."

The July before his death, he was persuaded to take a journey to Scarborough for the recovery of his health, from which he was at least encouraged to expect some little revival. After this he had thoughts of going to London, and intended to have spent part of September at Northampton. The expectation of this was mutually agreeable; but Providence saw fit to disconcert the scheme. His love for his friends in these parts occasioned him to express some regret on his being commanded back; and I am pretty confident, from the manner in which he expressed himself in one of his last letters to me, that he had some more important reasons for wishing an opportunity of making a London journey just at that crisis, which, the reader will remember, was before the rebellion broke out. But, as Providence determined it otherwise, he acquiesced; and I am well satisfied, that could he have distinctly foreseen the approaching event, so far as it concerned his own person, he would have esteemed it the happiest summons he ever received. While he was at Scarborough, I find by a letter dated from thence, July 26, 1745, that he had been informed of the gaiety which so unseasonably prevailed at Edinburgh, where great multitudes were then spending their time in balls, assemblies, and other gay amusements, little mindful of the rod of God which was then hanging over them; on which occasion he hath this expression: "I am greatly surprised that the people of Edinburgh should be employed in such foolish diversions, when our situation is at present more melancholy than ever I saw it in my life. But there is one thing which I am very sure of, and that comforts me, viz, that it shall go well with the righteous, come what will."

CHAPTER XV.

BATTLE OF PRESTONPANS.

QUICKLY after his return home, the flame burst out, and his regiment was ordered to Stirling. It was in that castle that his lady and eldest daughter enjoyed the last happy hours of his company, and I think it was about ten or twelve days before his death that he parted from them there. A remarkable circumstance attended that parting, which has been touched upon by surviving friends in more than one of their letters to me. His lady was so affected when she took her last leave of him, that she could not forbear bursting out into a flood of tears, with other marks of unusual emotion; and when he asked her the reason, she urged as a sufficient apology, the apprehension she had of losing such an invaluable friend, amidst the dangers to which he was then called out. On this she took particular notice, that whereas he had generally comforted her on such occasions by pleading with her that remarkable hand of Providence which had so frequently in former instances been exerted for his preservation, and that in the greatest extremity, he said nothing of it now; but only replied in his sententious manner, "We have an eternity to spend together."

That heroic contempt of death which had often discovered itself in the midst of former dangers, was manifested now in his discourse with several of his most intimate friends. I have reserved for this place one genuine expression of it many years before, which I thought might be mentioned with some advantage here. In July, 1725, he had been sent to some place not far from Hamilton to quell a mutiny among some of our troops. I know not the particular occasion; but I remember to have heard him mention it as so fierce a one, that he scarcely ever apprehended himself in more hazardous circumstances. Yet he quelled it by his presence alone, and the expostulations he used—evidently putting his life into his hand to do it. The particulars of the story struck me much; but I do not so exactly remember them as to venture to relate them here. I only observe, that in a letter dated July 16, that year, which I have now before me, and which evidently refers to this event, he writes thus: "I have been very busy, hurried about from place to place; but, blessed be God, all is over without bloodshed. And pray let me ask what made you show so much concern for me in your last? Were you afraid I should get to heaven before you? or can any evil befall those who are followers of that which is good?" *

As these were his sentiments in the vigour of his days, so neither did declining years and the infirmities of a broken constitution on the one hand, nor any desire of enjoying the honours and profits of so high a station, or (what was much more to him,) the converse of the most affectionate of wives and so many amiable children and friends on the other, in the least ener-

* I doubt not but this will remind some of my readers of that noble speech of Zuinglius, when (according to the usage of that country,) attending his flock to a battle in which their religion and liberties were all at stake, on his receiving a mortal wound by a bullet, of which he soon expired, while his friends were in all the first astonishment of grief, he bravely said, as he was dying, "*Ecquid hoc infortunii?* Is this to be reckoned a misfortune?" How many of our Deists would have celebrated such a sentence, if it had come from the lips of an ancient Roman! Strange that the name of Christ should be so odious, that the brightest virtues of his followers should be despised for his sake! But so it is, and so our Master told us it would be; and our faith is, in this connection, confirmed by those who strive most to overthrow it.

vate his spirits; but as he had in former years often expressed it, to me and several others, as his desire, "that if it were the will of God, he might have some honourable call to sacrifice his life in defence of religion and the liberties of his country;" so, when it appeared to him most probable that he might be called to it immediately, he met the summons with the greatest readiness. This appears in part from a letter which he wrote to the Rev. Mr. Adams, of Falkirk, just as he was marching from Stirling, which was only eight days before his death:—"The rebels," says he, "are advancing to cross the Frith; but I trust in the Almighty God, who doth whatsoever he pleases in the armies of heaven, and among the inhabitants of the earth." The same gentleman tells me, that, a few days after the date of this, he marched through Falkirk with his regiment; and though he was then in so languishing a state, that he needed his assistance as secretary to write for some reinforcements, which might put it in his power to make a stand, (as he was very desirous to have done,) he expressed a most genuine and noble contempt of life, when about to be exposed in the defence of a worthy cause.

These sentiments wrought in him to the last

in the most effectual manner, and he seemed for a while to have infused them into the regiment which he commanded; for they expressed such a spirit in their march from Stirling, that I am assured the colonel was obliged to exert all his authority to prevent their making incursions on the rebel army, which then lay very near him; and had it been thought proper to send him the reinforcements he requested, none can say what the consequence might have been; but he was ordered to march as fast as possible to meet Sir John Cope's forces at Dunbar, which he did; and that hasty retreat, in concurrence with the news which they soon after received of the surrender of Edinburgh to the rebels, (either by the treachery or weakness of a few, in opposition to the judgment of by far the greater and better part of the inhabitants,) struck a panic into both the regiments of dragoons, which became visible in some very apparent and remarkable circumstances in their behaviour, which I forbear to relate. This affected Colonel Gardiner so much that, on the Thursday before the fatal action of Prestonpans, he intimated to an officer of considerable rank and note, from whom I had it by a very sure channel of conveyance, that he expected the event would be as in fact it was. In this view, there is all imaginable reason to believe that he had formed his resolution as to his own personal conduct, which was, "that he would not, in case of the flight of those under his command, retreat with them;" by which, as it seemed, he was reasonably apprehensive that he might have stained the honour of his former services, and have given some occasion for the enemy to have spoken reproachfully. He much rather chose, if Providence gave him the call, to leave in his death an example of fidelity and bravery which might very probably be (as in fact it seems to have been) of much greater importance to his country than any other service which, in the few days of remaining life, he could expect to render it. I conclude these to have been his views, not only from what I knew of his general character and temper, but likewise from some intimations which he gave to a very worthy person from Edinburgh, who visited him the day before the action, and to whom he said, "I cannot influence the conduct of others as I could wish, but I have one life to sacrifice to my country's safety, and I shall not spare it,"—or words to that effect.

I have heard such a multitude of inconsistent reports of the circumstances of Colonel Gardiner's death, that I had almost despaired of being able to give my reader any particular satisfaction concerning so interesting a scene. But, by a happy accident, I have very lately had an opportunity of being exactly informed of the whole by that brave man, Mr. John Foster, his faithful servant, (and worthy of the honour of serving such a master,) whom I had seen with him at my house some years before. He attended him in his last hours, and gave me at large the narration, which he would be ready, if requisite, to attest upon oath. From his mouth I wrote it down with the utmost exactness, and could easily believe, from the genuine and affectionate manner in which he related the particulars, that according to his own striking expression, "his eye and his heart were always upon his honoured master during the whole time."*

* Just as I am putting the last hand to these memoirs, March 2, 1746-7, I have met with a corporal in Colonel Lascelles' regiment, who was an eye-witness to what happened at Prestonpans on the day of the battle, and the day before; and the account he has given me of some memorable particulars is so exactly agreeable to that which I received from Mr. Foster, that it would much corroborate his testimony, if there were not so many other considerations to render it convincing.

On Friday, 20th September, (the day before the battle which transmitted him to his immortal crown,) the colonel drew up his regiment in the afternoon, and rode through all their ranks, addressing them at once in the most respectful and animating manner, both as soldiers and as Christians, to exert themselves courageously in the service of their country, and to neglect nothing that might have a tendency to prepare them for whatever might happen. They seemed much affected with the address, and expressed a very ardent desire of attacking the enemy immediately—a desire in which he and another very gallant officer of distinguished rank, dignity, and character, both for bravery and conduct, would gladly have gratified them, if it had been in their power. He earnestly pressed it on the commanding officer, as the soldiers were then in better spirits than it could be supposed they would be after having passed the night under arms, and as the circumstance of making an attack would be some encouragement to them, and probably some terror to the enemy, who would have had the disadvantage of standing on the defence—a disadvantage with which those wild barbarians, (for such most of them were) perhaps would have been more struck than better disciplined troops—especially, too, when they fought against the laws of their country. He also apprehended that, by marching to meet them, some advantage might have been secured with regard to the ground, with which, it is natural to imagine, he must have been perfectly acquainted, as it lay just at his own door, and he had rode over it many hundred times. When I mention these things, I do not pretend to be capable of judging how far this advice was right. A variety of circumstances to me unknown might make it otherwise. It is certain, however, that it was brave. But it was overruled in this respect, as it also was in the disposition of the cannon, which he would have planted in the centre of our small army, rather than just before his regiment, which was in the right wing, where he was apprehensive that the horses, which had not been in any previous engagement, might be thrown into some disorder by the discharge so very near them. He urged this the more as he thought the attack of the rebels might probably be made on the centre of the foot, where he knew there were some brave men, on whose standing he thought, under God, the success of the day depended. When he found that he could not carry either of these points, nor some others which, out of regard to the common safety, he insisted upon with unusual earnestness, he dropped some intimations of the consequences he apprehended, and which did in fact follow; and submitting to Providence, spent the remainder of the day in making as good a disposition as circumstances would allow.*

He continued all night under arms, wrapt up in his cloak, and generally sheltered under a rick of barley which happened to be in the field. About three in the morning he called his domestic servants to him, of which there were four in waiting. He dismissed three of them with most affectionate Christian advice, and such solemn charges relating to the performance of

* Several of these circumstances have since been confirmed by the concurrent testimony of another very credible person, Mr. Robert Douglas, (now a surgeon in the navy,) who was a volunteer at Edinburgh just before the rebels entered the place, and who saw Colonel Gardiner come from Haddington to the field of battle the day before the action in a chaise, being (as from that circumstance he supposed) in so weak a state that he could not well endure the fatigue of riding on horseback. He observed Colonel Gardiner in discourse with several officers on the evening before the engagement, at which time, it was afterwards reported, he gave his advice to attack the rebels; and when it was overruled, he afterwards saw the colonel walk by himself in a very pensive manner.

their duty and the care of their souls, as plainly seemed to intimate that he at least apprehended it very probable he was taking his last farewell of them. There is great reason to believe that he spent the little remainder of the time, which could not be much above an hour, in those devout exercises of soul which had so long been habitual to him, and to which so many circumstances then concurred to call him.

The army was alarmed at break of day by the noise of the rebels' approach, and the attack was made before sunrise; yet it was light enough to discern what passed. As soon as the enemy came within gunshot, they made a furious fire; and it is said that the dragoons, which constituted the left wing, immediately fled. The colonel, at the beginning of the onset, which lasted but a few minutes, received a wound by a bullet in his left breast, which made him give a sudden spring in his saddle; upon which his servant, who had led the horse, would have persuaded him to retreat; but he said it was only a wound in the flesh, and fought on, though soon after he received a shot in his right thigh. In the meantime it was discovered that some of the enemies fell by him, particularly one man, who had made him a treacherous visit but a few days before, with great professions of zeal for the present establishment.

Events of this kind pass in less time than the description of them can be written, or than it can be read. The colonel was for a few moments supported by his men, and particularly by that worthy person, Lieutenant-colonel Whitney, who was shot through the arm, and who, a few months after, fell nobly in the battle of Falkirk; by Lieutenant West, a man of distinguished bravery; also by about fifteen dragoons, who stood by him to the last. But, after a faint fire, the regiment was seized with a panic; and though their colonel and some other gallant officers did what they could to rally them once or twice, they took to precipitate flight. Just at the moment when Colonel Gardiner seemed to be making a pause, to deliberate what duty required him to do in such a circumstance, an accident happened, which must, I think, in the judgment of every worthy and generous man, be deemed a sufficient apology for exposing his life to so great a hazard, when his regiment had left him.* He saw that a party of foot, who were

* The colonel, who was well acquainted with military history, might possibly remember that in the battle at Blenheim, the

then bravely fighting near him, and whom he was ordered to support, had no officer to head them; upon which he said eagerly, in the hearing of the person from whom I had this account, "Those brave fellows will be cut to pieces for want of a commander,"—or words to that effect. So saying, he rode up to them, and cried out aloud, "Fire on, my lads, and fear nothing." But, just as the words were out of his mouth, a Highlander advanced towards him with a scythe, fastened on a long pole, with which he gave him such a deep wound on his right arm, that his sword dropped out of his hand; and at the same time several others coming about him while he was thus dreadfully entangled with that cruel weapon, he was dragged off his horse. The moment he fell another Highlander, who, if the crown witness at Carlisle may be credited, (as I know not

illustrious Prince Eugene, when the horse of the wing which he commanded had run away thrice, charged at the head of the foot, and thereby greatly contributed to the glorious success of the day. At least such an example may conduce to vindicate that noble ardour which, amidst all the applauses of his country, some have been so cool and so critical as to blame. For my part, I thank God that I am not called to apologize for his following his troops in their flight, which I fear would have been a much harder task; and which, dear as he was to me, would have grieved me much more than his death, with these heroic circumstances attending it.

why he should not, though the unhappy creature died denying it,) was one M'Naught, who was executed about a year after, gave him a stroke either with a broadsword or a Lochaber axe, (for my informant could not exactly distinguish,) on the hinder part of his head, which was the mortal blow. All that his faithful attendant saw further at this time was, that as his hat had fallen off, he took it in his left hand, and waved it as a signal to him to retreat; and added, (the last words he ever heard him speak,) "Take care of yourself;" upon which the servant retired.

It was reported at Edinburgh, on the day of the battle, by what seemed a considerable authority, that as the colonel lay in his wounds, he said to a chief of the opposite side, "You are fighting for an earthly crown, I am going to receive a heavenly one,"—or something to that purpose. When I preached the sermon, long since printed, on occasion of his death, I had great reason to believe this report was true, though, before the publication of it, I began to be in doubt; and, on the whole, after the most accurate inquiry I could possibly make at this distance, I cannot get any convincing evidence of it. Yet I must here observe that it does not appear impossible that something of this kind might indeed be uttered by him, as his servant testifies that he spoke to him after receiving that fatal blow, which would seem most likely to have taken away the power of speech, and as it is certain he lived several hours after he fell. If, therefore, any thing of this kind did happen, it must have been just before this instant. But as to the story of his being taken prisoner and carried to the pretended Prince, (who, by the way, afterwards rode his horse, and entered into Derby upon it,) with several other circumstances which were grafted upon that interview, there is the most undoubted evidence of its falsehood; for his attendant above mentioned assures me that he himself immediately fled to a mill, at the distance of about two miles from the spot on which the colonel fell, where he changed his dress, and, disguised like a miller's servant, returned with a cart as soon as possible, which yet was not till nearly two hours after the engagement. The hurry of the action was then pretty well over, and he found his much-honoured master not only plundered of his watch and other things of value, but also stripped of his upper garments and boots, yet still breathing; and adds, that though he was not capable of speech, yet, on taking him up, he opened his eyes; which makes it something questionable whether he was altogether insensible. In this condition, and in this manner, he conveyed him to the church of Tranent, from whence he was immediately taken into the minister's house, and laid in bed, where he continued breathing and frequently groaning till about eleven in the forenoon, when he took his final leave of pain and sorrow, and undoubtedly rose to those distinguished glories which are reserved for those who have been eminently and remarkably faithful unto death.

From the moment he fell, it was no longer a battle, but a rout and carnage. The cruelties which the rebels (as it is generally said under the command of Lord Elcho,) inflicted on some of the king's troops after they had asked quarter, are dreadfully legible on the countenances of many who survived it. They entered Colonel Gardiner's house before he was carried off from the field, and notwithstanding the strict orders which the unhappy Duke of Perth (whose conduct is said to have been very humane in many instances,) gave to the contrary, every thing of value was plundered, to the very curtains of the beds, and hangings of the rooms. His papers were all thrown into the wildest disorder, and his house made an hospital for the reception of those who were wounded in the action.

Such was the close of a life which had been zealously devoted to God, and filled up with many honourable services. Such was the death of him who had been so highly favoured by God in the method by which he was brought back to him after so long and so great an estrangement, and in the progress of so many years, during which (in the expressive phrase of the most ancient of writers,) "he had walked with him;"—to fall, as God threatened the people of his wrath that they should do, "with tumult, with shouting, and with the sound of the trumpet." Amos ii. 2. Several other very worthy, and some of them very eminent persons, shared the same fate, either now at the battle of Prestonpans, or quickly after at that of Falkirk;* Providence, no doubt, permitting it, to establish our faith in the rewards of an invisible world, as well as to teach us to cease from man, and fix our dependence on an Almighty arm.

The remains of this Christian hero (as I be-

* Of these, none were more memorable than those illustrious brothers, Sir Robert Munro and Dr. Munro, whose tragical but glorious fate was also shared quickly after by a third hero of the family, Captain Munro, of Culcairn, brother to Sir Robert and the Doctor.

lieve every reader is now convinced he may justly be called,) were interred the Tuesday following, September 24, in the parish church at Tranent, where he had usually attended divine service, with great solemnity. His obsequies were honoured with the presence of some persons of distinction, who were not afraid of paying that mark of respect to his memory, though the country was then in the hands of the enemy. But, indeed, there was no great hazard in this; for his character was so well known, that even they themselves spoke honourably of him, and seemed to join with his friends in lamenting the fall of so brave and so worthy a man.

The remotest posterity will remember for whom the honour of subduing this unnatural and pernicious rebellion was reserved; and it will endear the Duke of Cumberland to all but the open or secret abettors of it in the present age, and consecrate his name to immortal honours among all the friends of religion and liberty who shall arise after us. And, I dare say, it will not be imagined that I at all derogate from his glory in suggesting, that the memory of that valiant and excellent person whose memoirs I am now concluding may in some measure have contributed to that signal and complete victory with which God was pleased to crown the arms of his Royal Highness; for the force of such an example is very animating, and a painful consciousness of having deserted such a commander in such extremity, must at least awaken, where there was any spark of generosity, an earnest desire to avenge his death on those who had sacrificed his blood, and that of so many other excellent persons, to the views of their ambition, rapine, or bigotry.

The reflections which I have made in my funeral sermon on my honoured friend, and in the dedication of it to his worthy and most afflicted lady, supersede many things which might otherwise have properly been added here. I conclude, therefore, with humbly acknowledging the wisdom and goodness of that awful Providence which drew so thick a gloom around him in the last hours of his life, that the lustre of his virtues might dart through it with a more vivid and observable ray. It is abundant matter of thankfulness that so signal a monument of grace, and ornament of the Christian profession, was raised in our age and country, and spared for so many honourable and useful years. Nor can all the tenderness of the most affectionate friendship, while its sorrows bleed afresh in the view of so tragical a scene, prevent my adoring the gracious appointment of the great Lord of all events, that when the day in which he must have expired without an enemy appeared so very near, the last ebb of his generous blood should be poured out, as a kind of sacred libation, to the liberties of his country, and the honour of his God! that all the other virtues of his character, embalmed as it were by that precious stream, might diffuse around a more extensive fragrance, and be transmitted to the most remote posterity with that peculiar charm which they cannot but derive from their connection with so gallant a fall—an event (as that blessed apostle, of whose spirit he so deeply drank, has expressed it) "according to his earnest expectation, and his hope that in him Christ might be glorified in all things, whether by his life or by his death."

THE COLONEL'S PERSONAL APPEARANCE.

In the midst of so many more important articles, I had really forgotten to say any thing of the person of Colonel Gardiner, of which, nevertheless, it may be proper here to add a word or two. He was, as I was informed, in younger life remarkably graceful and amiable; and I can easily believe it, from what I knew him to be when our acquaintance began, though he was then turned of fifty, and had gone through so many fatigues as well as dangers, which could not but leave some traces on his countenance. He was tall, (I suppose something more than six feet,) well proportioned, and strongly built; his eyes of a dark gray, and not very large; his forehead pretty high; his nose of a length and height no way remarkable, but very well suited to his other features; his cheeks not very prominent; his mouth moderately large, and his chin rather a little inclining (when I knew him) to be peaked. He had a strong voice and lively accent, with an air very intrepid, yet attempered with much gentleness. There was something in his manner of address most perfectly easy and obliging, which was in a great measure the result of the great candour and benevolence of his natural temper, and which, no doubt, was much improved by the deep humility which divine grace had wrought in his heart, as well as his having been accustomed from his early youth to the company of persons of distinguished rank and polite behaviour.

The picture of him, which is given at the beginning of these memoirs, was taken from an original done by Van Deest (a Dutchman brought into Scotland by general Wade,) in the year 1727, which was the 40th of his age, and is said to have been very like him then, though far from being an exact resemblance of what he was when I had the happiness of being acquainted with him.* Perhaps he would have appeared to the greatest advantage of all, could he have been exactly drawn on horseback; as many very good judges, and among the rest the celebrated Mons. Faubert himself, have spoken of him as one of the completest horsemen that has ever been known; and there was indeed something so singularly graceful in his appearance in that attitude, that it was sufficient (as what is very eminent in its kind generally is,) to strike an eye not formed on any critical rules.

* In presenting this likeness for the first time in an American edition of this work, the artist has taken the liberty to change the costume, by substituting the ordinary military dress for the court dress of the original.—*Editor of the Pres. Board of Publication.*

APPENDIX I.

(REFERRED TO ON PAGE 97.)

It may not be amiss, in illustration of Dr. Doddridge's remarks on the subject of dreams, to present to the reader the following account of a remarkable dream which occurred to the Doctor himself, and had a beneficial influence on his own mind.—ED. PRES. BD. PUB.

DR. DODDRIDGE'S DREAM.

Dr. Doddridge and Dr. Samuel Clark, of St. Alban's, having been conversing in the evening upon the nature of the separate state, and the probability that the scenes on which the soul would enter, at its first leaving the body, would have some resemblance to those things it had been conversant with while on earth, that it might by degrees be prepared for the more sublime happiness of the heavenly state, this and other conversation of the same kind probably occasioned the following dream.

The Doctor imagined himself dangerously ill at a friend's house in London, and after remaining in this state for some hours, he thought his soul left his body, and took its flight in some kind of a fine vehicle, though very different from the gross body it had just quitted, but still material. He pursued his course through the air, expecting some celestial messenger to meet him, till he was at some distance from the city, when turning back and viewing the town, he could not forbear saying to himself, "How vain do those affairs in which the inhabitants of this place are so eagerly employed, seem to me a separate spirit!" At length, as he was continuing his progress, though without any certain directions, yet easy and happy in the thoughts of the universal providence and government of God, which extends alike to all states and worlds, he was now met by one who told him he was sent to conduct him to his destined state of abode, from which he concluded it was an angel, though he appeared in the form of an elderly man. They accordingly advanced together, till they came within sight of a large spacious building, which had the air of a palace. Upon his inquiring what it was, his guide replied, it was the place assigned for him at present; upon which the Doctor wondered that he had read on earth, "that eye had not seen, nor ear had heard, the glory laid up for them that love God," when he could easily have formed an idea of such a building, from others he had seen, though he acknowledged they were greatly inferior to this in elegance and magnificence. The answer, his guide told him, was plainly suggested by the conversation of the evening before, and that the scenes presented to him were purposely contrived to bear a near resemblance to those he had been accustomed to on earth, that his mind might be more easily and gradually prepared for those glories which would open upon him hereafter, and which would at first have quite dazzled and overpowered him. By this time they came to the palace, and his guide led him through a kind of saloon into an inner parlour. The first object that struck him was a great golden cup which stood upon a table, on which was embossed the figure of a vine and clusters of grapes. He asked his guide the meaning of it; who told him that it was the cup in which his Saviour drank new wine with his disciples in his kingdom; and that the figures carved on it denoted the union between Christ and his Church, implying, that as the grapes derived all their beauty and flavour from the vine, so the saints, even in a state of glory, were indebted for their establishment in holiness and happiness, to their union with their common Head, in whom they are all complete. While they were conversing, he heard a tap at the door, and was informed by the angel that it was a signal of his Lord's approach, and was intended to prepare him for an interview. Accordingly, in a short time our Saviour entered the room, and upon his casting himself at his feet, he graciously raised him up, and with a smile of inexpressible complacency, assured him of his favour, and kind acceptance of his faithful services, and as a token of his peculiar regard, and the intimate friendship with which he intended to honour him, he took the cup, and after drinking of it himself, gave it into the Doctor's hand. The Doctor would have declined it at first, as too great an honour; but our Lord replied, as to Peter in washing his feet, "If thou drinkest not with me, thou hast no part with me." This he observed filled him with such a transport of gratitude, love and admiration, that he was ready to sink under it. His master seemed sensible of this, and told him he must leave him for the present, but would not be long before he repeated his visit. As soon as our Lord was retired, and the Doctor's mind more composed, he observed that the room was hung with pictures, and upon examining them, he found to his great surprise, that they contained all the history of his life; the most remarkable scenes he had passed through, being there represented in a very lively manner—the many temptations and trials he had been exposed to, and the signal instances of the divine goodness in the different periods of his life. It may not be easily imagined how this would strike and affect his mind. It excited in him the strongest emotions of gratitude, especially when he reflected that he was now out of the reach of any future danger, and that all the purposes of divine love towards him were so amply accomplished. The exstacy of joy and gratitude, into which these reflections threw him, was so great that he awoke; but for some time after he awoke the impression continued so lively that tears of joy flowed down his cheeks, and he said that he never, on any occasion, remembered to have had sentiments of devotion and love equal to it.

APPENDIX II.

(REFERRED TO ON PAGE 104.)

The following extract from Dr. Doddridge's "Thoughts on Sacramental Occasions," gives a beautiful and edifying picture of the exercises of his affectionate and pious heart under a painful bereavement.

THE SEVENTY-EIGHTH SACRAMENT, OCTOBER 3, 1736.

DEAR BETSEY DEAD.*

I had preached in the bitterness of my heart from these words: "Is it well with thy hus-

* The following extract from the Diary of Dr. Doddridge is here subjoined, as affording an explanation of some particulars alluded to in the text.

REFLECTIONS ON THE DEATH OF MY DEAR CHILD, AND THE MANY MOURNFUL PROVIDENCES ATTENDING IT.

I have a great deal of reason to condemn my own negligence and folly, that for so many months I have entered no memorandums of what has passed between God and my soul, although some of the transactions were very remarkable, as well as some things which I have heard concerning others; but the subject of this article is the most melancholy of any. We lost my dear and reverend brother and friend, Mr. Sanders, on the 31st of July last; on the 1st of September, Lady

band? is it well with the child? And she answered, It is well." 2 Kings iv. 26. I endeavoured to show the reason there was to say this; but surely there was never any dispensation of Providence in which I found it so hard,

Russel—that invaluable friend, died at Reading on her road from Bath; and on Friday, the 1st of October, God was pleased, by a most awful stroke, to take away my eldest, dearest child, my lovely Betsey. She was formed to strike my affections in the most powerful manner; such a person, genius, and temper, as I admired even beyond their real importance, so that indeed I doted upon her, and was for many months before her death in a great degree of bondage upon her account. She was taken ill at Newport about the middle of June, and from thence to the day of her death, she was my continual thought, and almost uninterrupted care. God only knows with what earnestness and importunity I prostrated myself before him to beg her life, which I would have been willing almost to have purchased with my own. When reduced to the lowest degree of languishment by a consumption, I could not forbear looking upon her almost every hour. I saw her with the strongest mixture of anguish and delight; no chemist ever watched his crucible with greater care, when he expected the production of the philosopher's stone, than I watched her in all the various turns of her distemper, which at last grew utterly hopeless, and then no language can express the agony into which it threw me. One remarkable circumstance I cannot but recollect: in praying most affectionately, perhaps too earnestly, for her life, these words came into my mind with great power, "Speak no more to me of this matter." I was unwilling to take them, and went into the chamber to see my dear lamb, when, instead of receiving me with her usual tenderness, she looked upon me with a stern air, and for my very soul had been overwhelmed within me. Indeed, some hard thoughts of the mercy of God were ready to arise; and the apprehension of his heavy displeasure, and the fear of my child's future state, added fuel to the fire.

said, with a very remarkable determination of voice, "I have no more to say to you;" and I think that from that time, although she lived at least ten days, she seldom looked upon me with pleasure, or cared to suffer me to come near her. But that I might feel all the bitterness of the affliction, Providence so ordered it, that I came in when her sharpest agonies were upon her, and those words, "O dear, O dear, what shall I do?" rung in my ears for succeeding hours and days. But God delivered her,— and she, without any violent pang in the article of her dissolution, quietly and sweetly fell asleep, as I hope, in Jesus, about ten at night, I being then at Maidwell. When I came home my mind was under a dark cloud relating to her eternal state; but God was pleased graciously to remove it, and gave me comfortable hopes, after having felt the most heart-rending sorrow. My dear wife bore the affliction in the most glorious manner, and discovered more wisdom, and piety, and steadiness of temper in a few days, than I had ever in six years an opportunity of observing before. O my soul, God has blasted thy gourd; thy greatest earthly delight is gone: seek it in heaven, where I hope this dear babe is; where I am sure that my Saviour is; and where I trust, through grace, notwithstanding all this irregularity of temper and of heart, that I shall shortly be.

Sunday, October 3, 1736.

FURTHER REFLECTIONS AFTRR THE FUNERAL OF MY DEAR BETSEY.

I have now been laying the delight of my eyes in the dust, and it is for ever hidden from them. My heart

Upon the whole, my mind was in the most painful agitation; but it pleased God, that, in composing the sermon, my soul became quieted, and I was brought into a more silent and cordial submission to the Divine will.

was too full to weep much. We had a suitable sermon from these words: "Doest thou well to be angry?" Jonah iv. 4; because of the gourd. I hope God knows that I am not angry; but sorrowful he surely allows me to be. I could have wished that more had been said concerning the hope we may have of our child; and it was a great disappointment to me that nothing of that kind should have been said by one that loved her so well as my brother Hunt did. Yet, I bless God, I have my hopes that she is lodged in the arms of Christ. And there was an occurrence that I took much notice of; I was most earnestly praying that God would be pleased to give me some further encouragement on this head, by letting some new light, or by directing me to some further thoughts upon the subject. Soon after, as I came into my wife's chamber, she told me that our maid Betty, who had indeed the affection of a parent for my dear girl, had just before assured her, that, on the Sabbath day evening, Betsey would be repeating to herself some things of what she had heard in my prayers and in my preachings, but did not care to talk of it to others; and my wife assured me that she solemnly recommended herself to God in the words that I had taught her a little before she died. Blessed God, hast thou not received her? I trust that thou hast, and pardoned the infirmities of her poor, short, childish, afflicted life. I hope, in some measure out of love to me, as thy servant, thou hast done it for Christ's sake; and I would consider the very hope, as an engagement to thy future service. Lord, I love those who were kind to my child, and wept with me for her; shall I not much more love

At the table I discoursed on these words, "Although my house be not so with God." 2 Samuel xxiii. 5. I observed, that domestic calamities may befall good men in their journey through life, and particularly in relation to their children; but that they have a refuge in God's covenant; it is everlasting; it is sure; it is well ordered—every provision is made according to our necessities; and shall be our salvation, as it is the object of our most affectionate regard.

One further circumstance I must record; and that is, that I here solemnly recollected that I had, in a former sacrament taken the cup with

thee, who, I hope, art at this moment taking care of her, and opening her infant faculties for the duties and blessedness of heaven.

Lord, I would consider myself as a dying creature. My first-born is gone;—my beloved child is laid in bed before me. I have often followed her to her bed in a literal sense; and shortly I shall follow her to that, where we shall lie down together, and our rest shall be together in the dust. In a literal sense the grave is ready for me. My grave is made—I have looked into it—a dear part of myself is already there; and when I stood at the Lord's table I stood directly over it. It is some pleasure to me to think that my dust will be lodged near that of my dear lamb, how much more to hope that my soul will rest with hers, and rejoice in her forever! But, O, let me not centre my thoughts even here; it is at rest with, and in God, that is my ultimate hope. Lord, may thy grace secure it to me! and in the mean time give me some holy acquiescence of soul in thee; and although my gourd be withered, yet shelter me under the shadow of thy wings.

October, 4, 1736.

these words, "Lord, I take this cup as a public and solemn token that I will refuse no other cup which thou shalt put into my hand." I mentioned this recollection, and charged it publicly on myself and my Christian friends. God has taken me at my word, but I do not retract it; I repeat it again with regard to every future cup.

I am just come from the coffin of my dear child, who seems to be sweetly asleep there, with a serene, composed, delightful countenance, once how animated with double life! There—lo! O my soul! lo there! is thine idol laid still in death—the creature which stood next to God in thine heart; to whom it was opened with a fond and flattering delight. Methinks I would learn to be dead with her—dead to the world. Oh that I could be dead with her, not any further than that her dear memory may promote my living to God.*

I had a great deal of very edifying conversation last night and this morning with my wife, whose wisdom does indeed make her face to shine under this affliction. She is supported and animated with a courage which seems not at all natural to her; talks with the utmost freedom, and has really said many of the most useful things that ever were said to me by any

* The following note was written in the margin of the manuscript by the late Rev. Thomas Stedman: "I think I have heard that the doctor wrote his funeral sermon for his daughter, or a part of it, upon her coffin."

person upon the earth, both as to consolation and admonition. Had the best things I have read on the subject been collected together, they could hardly have been better conceived or better expressed. This is to me very surprising, when I consider her usual reserve. I have all imaginable reason to believe that God will make this affliction a great blessing to her, and I hope it may prove so to me. There was a fond delight and complacence which I took in Betsey beyond any thing living. Although she had not a tenth part of that rational, manly love, which I pay to her mamma, and many surviving friends; yet it leaves a peculiar pain upon my heart, and it is almost as if my very gall were poured out upon the earth. Yet much sweetness mingles itself with this bitter potion, chiefly in the view and hope of my speedy removal to the eternal world. May it not be the beauty of this providence, that instead of her living many years upon the earth, God may have taken away my child that I might be fitted for and reconciled to my own dissolution, perhaps nearly approaching? I verily believe that I shall meet her there, and enjoy much more of her in heaven than I should have done had she survived me on earth. Lord, thy will be done; may my life be used for the service while continued, and then put thou a period to it whenever thou pleasest.

www.ingramcontent.com/pod-product-compliance
Lightning Source LLC
LaVergne TN
LVHW050529100826
845148LV00002B/489